READING
COMPREHENSION

Verbal Preparation Guide

This in-depth guide takes the mystery out of complex reading passages by providing a toolkit of sketching techniques that aim to build comprehension, speed, and accuracy. Learn to identify the underlying structure of reading passages and develop methods to tackle the toughest comprehension questions.

Reading Comprehension GMAT Preparation Guide, 2007 Edition

10-digit International Standard Book Number: 0-9790175-6-4
13-digit International Standard Book Number: 978-0-9790175-6-8

8 GUIDE INSTRUCTIONAL SERIES

Math GMAT Preparation Guides

Number Properties (ISBN: 978-0-9790175-0-6)

Fractions, Decimals, & Percents (ISBN: 978-0-9790175-1-3)

Equations, Inequalities, & VIC's (ISBN: 978-0-9790175-2-0)

Word Translations (ISBN: 978-0-9790175-3-7)

Geometry (ISBN: 978-0-9790175-4-4)

Verbal GMAT Preparation Guides

Critical Reasoning (ISBN: 978-0-9790175-5-1)

Reading Comprehension (ISBN: 978-0-9790175-6-8)

Sentence Correction (ISBN: 978-0-9790175-7-5)

HOW OUR GMAT PREP BOOKS ARE DIFFERENT

One of our core beliefs at Manhattan GMAT is that a curriculum should be more than just a guidebook of tricks and tips. Scoring well on the GMAT requires a curriculum that builds true content knowledge and understanding. Skim through this guide and this is what you will see:

You will *not* find page after page of guessing techniques.

Instead, you will find a highly organized and structured guide that actually teaches you the content you need to know to do well on the GMAT.

You *will* find many more pages-per-topic than in all-in-one tomes.

Each chapter covers one specific topic area in-depth, explaining key concepts, detailing in-depth strategies, and building specific skills through Manhattan GMAT's *In-Action* problem sets (with comprehensive explanations). Why are there 8 guides? Each of the 8 books (5 Math, 3 Verbal) covers a major content area in extensive depth, allowing you to delve into each topic in great detail. In addition, you may purchase only those guides that pertain to those areas in which you need to improve.

This guide is challenging - it asks you to do more, not less.

It starts with the fundamental skills, but does not end there; it also includes the *most advanced content* that many other prep books ignore. As the average GMAT score required to gain admission to top business schools continues to rise, this guide, together with the 6 computer adaptive online practice exams and bonus question bank included with your purchase, provides test-takers with the depth and volume of advanced material essential for achieving the highest scores, given the GMAT's computer adaptive format.

This guide is ambitious - developing mastery is its goal.

Developed by Manhattan GMAT's staff of REAL teachers (all of whom have 99th percentile official GMAT scores), our ambitious curriculum seeks to provide test-takers of all levels with an in-depth and carefully tailored approach that enables our students to achieve mastery. If you are looking to learn more than just the "process of elimination" and if you want to develop skills, strategies, and a confident approach to any problem that you may see on the GMAT, then our sophisticated preparation guides are the tools to get you there.

HOW TO ACCESS YOUR ONLINE RESOURCES

Please read this entire page of information, all the way down to the bottom of the page! This page describes WHAT online resources are included with the purchase of this book and HOW to access these resources.

[**If you are a registered Manhattan GMAT student** and have received this book as part of your course materials, you have AUTOMATIC access to ALL of our online resources. This includes all simulated practice exams, question banks, and online updates to this book. To access these resources, follow the instructions in the Welcome Guide provided to you at the start of your program. Do NOT follow the instructions below.]

If you have purchased this book, your purchase includes 1 YEAR OF ONLINE ACCESS to the following:

> **6 Computer Adaptive Online Practice Exams**

> **Bonus Online Question Bank for READING COMPREHENSION**

> **Online Updates to the Content in this Book**

The 6 full-length computer adaptive practice exams included with the purchase of this book are delivered online using Manhattan GMAT's proprietary computer adaptive online test engine. The exams adapt to your ability level by drawing from a bank of more than 1200 unique questions of varying difficulty levels written by Manhattan GMAT's expert instructors, all of whom have scored in the 99th percentile on the Official GMAT. At the end of each exam you will receive a score, an analysis of your results, and the opportunity to review detailed explanations for each question. You may choose to take the exams timed or untimed.

The Bonus Online Question Bank for Reading Comprehension consists of 25 extra practice questions (with detailed explanations) that test the variety of Reading Comprehension concepts and skills covered in this book. These questions provide you with extra practice *beyond* the problem sets contained in this book. You may use our online timer to practice your pacing by setting time limits for each question in the bank.

The content presented in this book is updated periodically to ensure that it reflects the GMAT's most current trends. You may view all updates, including any known errors or changes, upon registering for online access.

Important Note: The 6 computer adaptive online exams included with the purchase of this book are the SAME exams that you receive upon purchasing ANY book in Manhattan GMAT's 8 Book Preparation Series. On the other hand, the Bonus Online Question Bank for READING COMPREHENSION is a unique resource that you receive ONLY with the purchase of this specific title.

To access the online resources listed above, you will need this book in front of you and you will need to register your information online. This book includes access to the above resources for ONE PERSON ONLY.

To register and start using your online resources, please go online to the following URL:

http://www.manhattangmat.com/access.cfm   (Double check that you have typed this in accurately!)

Your one-year of online access begins on the day that you register at the above URL. You only need to register your product ONCE at the above URL. To use your online resources any time AFTER you have completed the registration process, please login to the following URL:

http://www.manhattangmat.com/practicecenter.cfm

TABLE OF CONTENTS

g

Chapter 1

of

READING COMPREHENSION

INTRODUCTION TO PASSAGES & METHODS

In This Chapter . . .

- Reading Passage Features
- The Problem: You Read It But Don't Understand It
- The Solution: Don't Just Read, Do Something!

READING PASSAGE FEATURES

Reading Comprehension questions are generally familiar to most students from other standardized tests. You are shown a passage that consists of two or more paragraphs and asked questions that require you to understand the substance of the passage.

You can expect to see **4** Reading Comprehension passages on the GMAT. Each passage will typically be accompanied by 3 to 4 questions, for a total of 12 to 14 Reading Comprehension questions.

There are a number of features related to GMAT Reading Comprehension passages that you should be aware of:

All Passages are either Long or Short. GMAT Reading Comprehension passages come in two basic forms: LONG and SHORT. Long passages generally consist of four to five short paragraphs or three medium-length paragraphs, and are more than 50 lines on the computer screen in length (or over 35 lines in *The Official Guide for GMAT Review, 11th Edition* and *The Official Guide for GMAT Verbal Review*). Examples of long passages on the GMAT appear on pages 346, 350, and 360 of *The Official Guide for GMAT Review, 11th Edition.*

Short passages generally consist of two or three short paragraphs, and are fewer than 50 lines on the computer screen in length (or under 35 lines in *The Official Guide for GMAT Review, 11th Edition* and *The Official Guide for GMAT Verbal Review*). Examples of short passages on the GMAT appear on pages 348, 352, and 354 of *The Official Guide for GMAT Review, 11th Edition.* It is important to immediately recognize whether a passage is Long or Short, as one's approach to each type of passage should be different.

Short passages have been more common on the GMAT in the past several years than Long passages. Of the four passages that you see on the GMAT, 3 of them are likely to be Short and 1 of them Long. However, there is no set order in the appearance of Short and Long passages.

Questions Appear One at a Time. Due to the computerized format of the exam, the questions are presented one at a time on the right side of the computer screen, while the complete reading passage remains on the left side of the screen throughout. Since questions are presented one at a time, and you cannot return to any question after answering it, you will only be able to see the first question prior to reading the passage.

The Number of Questions per Passage is NOT stated. The GMAT does NOT indicate how many questions are associated with a particular passage (i.e. there is NO language on the GMAT indicating that "Questions 6-9 refer to the following passage."). However, there is a very strong correlation between the length of the passage and the number of questions associated with it. Generally, each Short passage will have 3 questions associated with it, and each Long passage will have 4 questions associated with it. This is one reason why it is important to recognize whether a passage is Long or Short.

In order to determine your reading approach, first identify whether a passage is Long or Short.

Line Numbers are Not Listed. Though the Official Guide and older GMAT tests list line numbers down the side of each paragraph, the GMAT now does not number the lines in each passage. If a GMAT question wants to indicate the location of a particular term or phrase in the passage, it will highlight that term in the passage text as the question appears.

We will discuss other features of GMAT Reading Comprehension passages and questions in the sections that follow.

The Problem: You Read It But Don't Understand It

Most people, when reading a GMAT Reading Comprehension passage, have an experience something like this:

Unlike the *Official Guide For GMAT Review*, the GMAT exam will NOT indicate how many questions to expect for a given passage.

> You quickly read the first paragraph of the passage. You then scan the second and third paragraphs, which blend into the first paragraph. After a couple of minutes spent reading, you finish the passage and turn to the first question.
>
> You understand what you have just read in a general way, but not to a level where you have confidence to answer the first question right away. You are forced to re-read the parts of the passage that you think are relevant to the first question. After you re-read these sections a couple of times, your understanding builds to a point that you feel you can answer the question.
>
> You repeat this process for each question. Often, you answer every question that relates to a particular passage without ever feeling like you understood the passage.

Most individuals, when faced with a Reading Comprehension passage, simply read the passage and then try to answer the relevant questions. There are several potential problems with this approach, but the main problem is that the time spent initially reading the passage is unproductive and does not facilitate genuine comprehension. As a result, one must essentially re-read the passage several times to answer even general questions about the passage.

This is primarily a function of how reading and understanding relate to each other. Reading words and understanding the substance of the the sentences or paragraphs that they form are very different processes. The vast majority of people cannot understand the substance of academic prose by simply reading words on a page or screen.

INTRODUCTION TO PASSAGES & METHODS   **Chapter 1**

The Solution: Don't Just Read, Do Something!

There are three general methods that we use to learn something new:

1. We read, as when we read a college textbook (or this guide).
2. We write, as when we take notes during a college lecture.
3. We listen, as during a lecture in a college course.

On the GMAT, we are asked to quickly read and synthesize passages of text. However, it is possible to build your comprehension more quickly by incorporating more than one learning method into your approach to these passages.

The key to quickly building comprehension is to WRITE something as you read. If you write down certain key elements as you read, you will build your understanding of each passage much more quickly and thoroughly. Writing activates a second learning process that facilitates comprehension. Identifying and writing elements of the passage will force you to read ACTIVELY as opposed to passively, dramatically improving the pace and depth of your comprehension.

Of course, it is not possible to re-write an entire passage in the time allocated for Reading Comprehension questions. But even writing and summarizing selected key elements will give you an understanding of the structure and main points of a passage while saving you time to answer questions about the passage.

During the chapters ahead you will learn WHAT to write down as you read a GMAT reading passage.

Become an ACTIVE reader by writing as you read each passage.

*Manhattan*GMAT*Prep
the new standard   15

Chapter 2
of
READING COMPREHENSION

SHORT
PASSAGES

In This Chapter . . .

SHORT PASSAGES: AN OVERVIEW

Because Short passages generally appear more often on the GMAT, we will discuss them first. Recall that Short passages consist of two or three paragraphs, and are fewer than 50 lines on the computer screen in length (or under 35 lines in *The Official Guide for GMAT Review, 11th Edition* and *The Official Guide for GMAT Verbal Review*).

All passages on the GMAT relate to one of three topic areas: Social Science, Science, or Business. Although these topics can be interesting, the GMAT makes them as boring and tedious as possible by using dry, clinical language, replete with long, detail-laden sentences.

The basic problem with each Short passage is that, despite the passage's relative brevity, there is too much information to absorb in one sustained reading. Additionally, there is not enough time to outline the entire passage, with all its details and nuances.

Moreover, without knowing what all of the questions are in advance (recall that you will only see the first question prior to reading the passage), it is impossible to know what to focus on in an initial reading.

The solution is to create a HEADLINE LIST of the passage during your first reading. A Headline List serves several purposes:

> (1) It fosters an understanding of the content and purpose of the passage by using writing to promote active reading.

> (2) It provides a general structure without getting bogged down in details.

> (3) It promotes a fast first reading of a passage that will still allow ample time to be spent on answering questions.

> Creating a Headline List for a Short passage builds comprehension and promotes speed without getting bogged down in the details.

The Headline List

The creation of a Headline List has several key elements:

(1) Just as a headline summarizes and conveys the main idea of a newspaper article, so too should your Headline List summarize the main idea of each paragraph.

Each paragraph has one topic sentence that gives the main point of the paragraph. Generally, the topic sentence is the first or second sentence, although it can also be a combination of the two.

Identify the topic sentence of the first paragraph. After you have identified the topic sentence, summarize it concisely on your scratch paper in the form of a headline. If you cannot identify a topic sentence, then your headline should be one sentence that concisely summarizes the main idea(s) of the paragraph (which will generally be the combination of two sentences).

(2) Approach the rest of the paragraph with an eye for key words.

You should continue to quickly read the first paragraph sentence-by-sentence, and briefly summarize any other point in the first paragraph that is important and distinct from the topic sentence that you have identified. Often, this will consist of simply jotting down a key word or example. Any identified key words should be indented and bulleted beneath the headline for the paragraph.

Follow the same process for any subsequent paragraphs, generating a headline and key-words for each. Short passages are organized such that each paragraph may introduce a whole new idea. Therefore, the approach to each subsequent paragraph should be the same as with the first paragraph.

Practice developing your own shorthand notation for your Headline Lists.

Notations In Your Headline List

There are certain notations that you should use to make creating your Headline List as time-efficient as possible:

(1) Abbreviate long terms, particularly proper nouns. Capitalize any abbreviations to ensure that the abbreviation is clear.

(2) Cause and Effect Statements are particularly common relationships. Use arrows (e.g. →) to indicate the cause leading to the effect.

(3) If a passage contains speakers, writers, points-of-view, arguments, etc., keep them organized by placing the person with the opinion before a given opinion with a colon. For example: **Historians: economic interests led to the war.**

(4) If examples are used, list them in parentheses. For example: **Insects are inflexible (sphex wasp).**

You may develop certain individual notations on your own in addition to those listed above, but practice your techniques and keep them CONSISTENT.

Some students may benefit from more visually-oriented sketching approaches that are less text-based and more graphic in nature (e.g. utilizing pictures). It is appropriate to use these approaches, as long as you practice with them extensively so that you are comfortable using them on exam day.

Answering Questions with Your Headline List

How is the Headline List used in answering the questions asked about a Short passage?

The Headline List provides ready-made answers to all GENERAL question types. These are questions that pertain to the main idea of the passage, the purpose of the passage, and the structure or form of the passage, as well as questions that relate to the author's style and objectives. The first question, which is visible along with the passage initially, is often a General question.

General questions can be answered directly by reviewing your Headline List. More importantly, the act of producing the Headline List (summarizing topic sentences and identifying key points) promotes understanding that should make answering GENERAL questions relatively straightforward.

The Headline List also provides a search tool for answering all SPECIFIC questions. These are detail-oriented questions, which can only be answered by returning to the text of the passage. Using your Headline List, and your understanding of the passage, you can quickly determine which paragraph you need to read in order to find a particular detail. Often a Specific question will refer to a key word that you have jotted down on your Headline List.

Using your Headline List to answer questions will be discussed further in the next section on Question Types.

Timing for Short Passages

In general, you have approximately one minute and forty-five seconds per question on the GMAT Verbal section, but you should plan on taking a little bit more time on Reading Comprehension questions.

A good rule to determine how much time to spend on a particular passage is as follows:

(Approximate # of Expected Questions) x 2 = Total # of Minutes You Should Spend

This total number of minutes includes time for both reading the passage, creating a headline list and answering all the questions.

Typically, each Short passages has 3 questions associated with it. Thus, you have roughly **6 minutes** to read and sketch the Short passage and then answer the associated questions.

Of this 6 minutes, approximately 2 to 2.5 minutes should be spent reading and generating your Headline List, with between 60 and 90 seconds actually spent answering each question. The first question will often be a General question; you should try to answer General questions within 60 seconds. Specific questions will be more time-consuming as they demand that you review the text of the passage; you should allocate up to 90 seconds for any Specific question.

Using Headline Lists is best learned by repeated practice. The sample Short passages that follow are accompanied by model Headline Lists.

> Spend approximately 6 minutes reading, creating a Headline List, and answering all the questions for a given Short passage.

Model Short Passage: *Insect Behavior*

Insect behavior generally appears to be explicable in terms of unconscious stimulus-response mechanisms; when scrutinized, it often reveals a stereotyped, inflexible quality. A classic example is the behavior of the female sphex wasp. In a typical case, the mother leaves her egg sealed in a burrow alongside a paralyzed grasshopper, which her larva can eat when it hatches. Before she deposits the grasshopper in the burrow, she leaves it at the entrance and goes inside to inspect the burrow. If the inspection reveals no problems, she drags the grasshopper inside by its antennae. Scientific experiments have uncovered an inability on the wasp's part to change its behavior when experiencing disruptions of this routine.

Charles Darwin discovered that if the grasshopper's antennae are removed the wasp will not drag it into the burrow, even though the legs or ovipositor could serve the same function as the antennae. Later Jean-Henri Fabre found more evidence of the wasp's dependence on pre-determined routine. While a wasp was performing her inspection of a burrow, he moved the grasshopper a few centimeters away from the burrow's mouth. The wasp brought the grasshopper back to the edge of the burrow, then began a whole new inspection. When Fabre took this opportunity to move the food again, the wasp repeated her routine. Fabre performed his disruptive maneuver forty times, and the wasp's response never changed.

> If a paragraph in a Short passage does not have one topic sentence, create headlines for the main points of that paragraph instead.

Model Headline List for *Insect Behavior*

> Insect behavior: displays unconscious stimulus-response mechanisms, inflexible quality
>   --(female sphex wasp)
>   --Experiments show inability to change routine
>
> D: discovered wasp won't drag grasshopper if no antennae
> Later, F: found more evidence of dependence upon routine

The topic sentence of the first paragraph is summarized, and other important points from the first paragraph are briefly listed. Notice that there is not one topic sentence in the second paragraph so the Headline List summarizes the paragraph's two main points instead.

Model Short Passage: *Animal Treatment*

Over the course of the eighteenth and early nineteenth centuries, educated Britons came to embrace the notion that animals must be treated humanely. By 1822 Parliament had outlawed certain forms of cruelty to domestic animals, and by 1824 reformers had founded the Society for the Prevention of Cruelty to Animals.

This growth in humane feelings was part of a broader embrace of compassionate ideals. One of the great movements of the age was abolitionism, but there were many other such causes. In 1785 a Society for the Relief of Persons Imprisoned for Small Sums persuaded Parliament to limit that archaic punishment. There was also a Society for Bettering the Condition of the Poor, founded in 1796. A Philanthropic Society founded in 1788 provided for abandoned children. Charity schools, schools of midwifery, and hospitals for the poor were being endowed. This growth in concern for human suffering encouraged reformers to reject animal suffering as well.

Industrialization and the growth of towns also contributed to the increase in concern for animals. The people who protested against cruelty to animals tended to be city folk who thought of animals as pets rather than as livestock. It was not just animals, but all of nature that came to be seen differently as Britain industrialized. Nature was no longer a menacing force that had to be subdued, for society's "victory" over wilderness was conspicuous everywhere. A new sensibility, which viewed animals and wild nature as things to be respected and preserved, replaced the old adversarial relationship. Animals, indeed, were to some extent romanticized as emblems of a bucolic, pre-industrial age.

Practice creating Headline Lists for all the Short passages contained in *The Official Guide for GMAT Review*.

Model Headline List for *Animal Treatment*

18th and early 19th centuries, educated Bs believe animal cruelty bad

Part of broad embrace of compassion
    --(slaves, poor, children)

Industrialization and growth of towns → concern for animals
    --Nature romanticized

The topic sentence of the first paragraph is summarized. The topic sentences of the second and third paragraphs are then summarized, with notable examples listed beneath.

Chapter 3
of
READING COMPREHENSION

LONG
PASSAGES

In This Chapter . . .

LONG PASSAGES: AN OVERVIEW

Recall that Long passages generally consist of four to five short paragraphs or three medium-length paragraphs, and are more than 50 lines on the computer screen in length (or over 35 lines in *The Official Guide for GMAT Review, 11th Edition* and *The Official Guide for GMAT Verbal Review*).

You will generally see 1 Long passage per GMAT exam, though you may see as many as 2. Each Long passage will typically have 4 questions associated with it, although this may also vary.

Long passages present all of the problems as Short passages, only more so. There is far too much information to absorb in one sustained reading. There is not enough time to outline the entire passage. Without knowing what all of the questions are, it is impossible to know what to focus on in an initial reading. Finally, the length of the passage makes answering specific questions particularly difficult, because it is often challenging to locate the relevant text.

The solution is to create a SKELETAL SKETCH of the passage. As with the Headline List for short passages, a Skeletal Sketch serves several purposes:

> (1) It fosters an understanding of the content and purpose of the passage by using writing to promote active reading.

> (2) It provides a general structure without getting bogged down in details.

> (3) It promotes a fast first reading of a long, complex passage that will still allow ample time to be spent on answering questions.

The Skeletal Sketch

The creation of a Skeletal Sketch has several key elements:

(1) Just as the top of a skeleton (the skull) is its most defined feature, so too the first paragraph of every Long passage gives shape to the text. As such, your Skeletal Sketch requires a defined "skull."

The primary difference between a Long passage and a Short passage is that, with a Long Passage, the first paragraph is generally the key to understanding the rest of the passage. Thus, you should take some extra time to summarize and make sure that you thoroughly understand the main points of the first paragraph.

To form the skull, you should read the first sentence of the first paragraph. After you have read it, summarize it concisely on your scratch paper. You should continue to read the first paragraph sentence-by-sentence, and summarize **every** sentence in the first paragraph. After you have done so, underline what you determine to be the main idea of the passage.

> The Skeletal Sketch emphasizes the first paragraph, or skull, and de-emphasizes the details contained in subsequent paragraphs.

(2) The limbs of your Skeletal Sketch are one-sentence summaries of each of the remaining paragraphs.

The subsequent paragraphs of a Long passage are not as important as the first. As a result, you should read these paragraphs differently than you read the first paragraph.

Read each paragraph with one aim in mind: to determine the main point or purpose of the paragraph. Focus your reading on the first one or two sentences of the paragraph, as this is usually where the paragraph's topic is found.

Read all the remaining sentences very quickly, intentionally skimming over details and examples. There is no point in trying to absorb the nitty-gritty details embedded in these sentences during this initial reading; if you are asked a specific detail question, you will need to re-read these sentences later anyway. In fact it is *counter-productive* to try to absorb these details since it takes you away from the main goal of your initial reading and sketching, that of understanding the overall structure of the passage.

After you have read a paragraph, summarize its purpose and main point in one sentence and write this sentence beneath the Skull. Then move on to the next paragraph and do the same. These one-sentence summaries are the limbs of your Skeletal Sketch.

You should use the same set of notations as discussed for Short passages.

> During your initial reading of the passage, identify the main idea of each body paragraph without getting bogged down in the details.

Answering Questions with Your Skeletal Sketch

How is the Skeletal Sketch used in answering the questions asked about a Long passage?

The Skeletal Sketch provides ready-made answers to all GENERAL question types. These are questions that pertain to the main idea of the passage, the purpose of the passage, and the structure or form of the passage, as well as questions that relate to the author's style and objectives. The first question, which is visible along with the passage initially, is often a General question.

General questions can be answered directly by reviewing your Skeletal Sketch. More importantly, the act of producing the Skeletal Sketch promotes comprehension that should help you answer general questions without referring back to the text of the passage itself.

The Skeletal Sketch also provides a search tool for answering all SPECIFIC questions. These are detail-oriented questions, which can only be answered by returning to the text of the passage. Using the limbs (the one sentence summaries) of your Skeletal Sketch, you can determine which paragraph you need to read in order to find a particular detail.

Using your sketch to answer questions will be discussed further in the next section on Question Types.

Timing for Long Passages

Recall from our discussion of Short passages the following rule to determine how much time to spend on a particular reading passage:

(Approximate # of Expected Questions) x 2 = Total # of Minutes You Should Spend

This total number of minutes includes time for both reading the passage, creating a Skeletal Sketch, and answering all the questions.

Typically, each Long passages has 4 questions associated with it. Thus, you have roughly **8 minutes** to read and sketch the Long passage and then answer the associated questions.

Of these 8 minutes, approximately 3 minutes should be spent reading and generating your Skeletal Sketch, with between 60 and 90 seconds actually spent answering each question. The first question will often be a General question; you should try to answer General questions within 60 seconds. Specific questions will be more time-consuming as they demand that you review the text of the passage; you should allocate up to 90 seconds for any Specific question.

Using Skeletal Sketches is best learned by repeated practice. The sample Long passages that follow are accompanied by model Skeletal Sketches.

Spend approximately 8 minutes reading, creating a Skeletal Sketch, and answering all the questions for a given Long passage.

Model Long Passage: *Electroconvulsive Therapy*

By skimming over the details and thereby saving time, you should be able to read and sketch a Long passage in roughly 3 minutes.

Electroconvulsive therapy (ECT) is a controversial psychiatric treatment involving the induction of a seizure in a patient by passing electricity through the brain. While beneficial effects of electrically induced seizures are evident and predictable in most patients, a unified mechanism of action has not yet been established and remains the subject of numerous investigations. ECT is extremely effective against severe depression, some acute psychotic states, and mania, though, like many medical procedures, it has its risks.

Since the inception of ECT in 1938, the public has held a strongly negative conception of the procedure. Initially, doctors employed unmodified ECT. Patients were rendered instantly unconscious by the electrical current, but the strength of the muscle contractions from uncontrolled motor seizures often led to compression fractures of the spine or damage to the teeth. In addition to the effect this physical trauma had on public sentiment, graphic examples of abuse in books and movies, such as Ken Kesey's *One Flew Over the Cuckoo's Nest*, portrayed ECT as punitive, cruel, overused, and violative of patients' legal rights.

Modern ECT is virtually unrecognizable from its earlier days. The treatment is modified by the muscle relaxant succinylcholine, which renders muscle contractions virtually nonexistent. Additionally, patients are given a general anesthetic. Thus, the patient is asleep and fully unaware during the procedure, and the only outward sign of a seizure may be the rhythmic movement of the patient's hand or foot. ECT is generally used in severely depressed patients for whom psychotherapy and medication prove ineffective. It may also be considered when there is an imminent risk of suicide, since antidepressants often take several weeks to work effectively. Exactly how ECT exerts its effects is not known, but repeated applications affect several neurotransmitters in the brain, including serotonin, norepinephrine, and dopamine.

ECT has proven effective, but it is not without controversy. Though decades-old studies showing brain cell death have been refuted in recent research, many patients do report loss of memory for events that occurred in the days, weeks or months surrounding the ECT. Some patients have also reported that their short-term memories continue to be affected for months after ECT, though some doctors argue that this may reflect the type of amnesia sometimes associated with severe depression.

Model Skeletal Sketch: *Electroconvulsive Therapy*

<u>ECT: controv psych. treatment, electr. into brain to induce seizure</u>
--beneficial effects, but no unified mechanism of action
--works for severe depress, some psych. states, mania; has risks

Since inception in 1938, public dislikes ECT

Modern ECT totally different, modified treatment

ECT effective, but controversial due to memory loss issues

The limbs of your
sketch are concise
one-line summaries of
each body paragraph.

Notice that the "skull" of the sketch includes the most detail, as it carefully outlines the major points of the first paragraph.

The limbs of the sketch are each very concise, consisting only of a brief summary of the main idea of each body paragraph. Note that for each of the body paragraphs, the main idea, as is usually the case, is found in the first one or two sentences of the paragraph.

Model Long Passage: *Ether's Existence*

Practice creating
Skeletal Sketches for
all the Long passages
contained in *The
Official Guide for
GMAT Review*.

In 1887, an ingenious experiment performed by Albert Michelson and Edward Morley severely undermined classical physics by failing to confirm the existence of "ether", a ghostly massless medium that was thought to permeate the universe. This finding had profound results, ultimately paving the way for acceptance of Einstein's special theory of relativity.

Prior to the Michelson-Morley experiment, nineteenth-century physics conceived of light as a wave propagated at constant speed through the ether. The existence of ether was hypothesized in part to explain the transmission of light, which was believed to be impossible through "empty" space. Physical objects, such as planets, were also thought to glide frictionlessly through the unmoving ether.

The Michelson-Morley experiment relied on the fact that the Earth, which orbits the Sun, would have to be in motion relative to a fixed ether. Just as a person on a motorcycle experiences a "wind" caused by her own motion relative to the air, the Earth would experience an "ethereal wind" caused by its motion through the ether. Such a wind would affect our measurements of the speed of light. If the speed of light is fixed with respect to the ether, but the earth is moving through the ether, then to an observer on Earth light must appear to move faster in a "downwind" direction than in an "upwind" direction.

In 1887 there were no clocks sufficiently precise to detect the speed differences that would result from an ethereal wind. Michelson and Morley surmounted this problem by using the wavelike properties of light itself to test for such speed differences. In their apparatus, known as an "interferometer", a single beam of light is split in half. Mirrors guide each half of the beam along a separate trajectory, before ultimately reuniting the two half-beams into a single beam. If one half-beam has moved more slowly than the other, the reunited beams will be out of phase with each other. In other words, peaks of the first half-beam will not coincide exactly with peaks of the second half-beam, resulting in an interference pattern in the reunited beam. Michelson and Morley detected only a tiny degree of interference in the reunited light beam - far less than what was expected based on the motion of the Earth.

Model Skeletal Sketch: *Ether's Existence*

<u>1887, M + M experiment → undermined classical physics, no ether</u>
--ether = medium permeating the universe
--Important finding → acceptance of E's theory

Before M + M, 19th C. physics: light = wave propagated through ether

M + M experiment relied on fact that Earth would have to be in motion through ether, causing ethereal "wind" (like wind on motorcycle)

M + M tested for speed differences that would result from ethereal wind; found far less interference than expected

The main idea of a paragraph is usually found in the first or second sentence.

The "skull" of this sketch summarizes the brief first paragraph. The limbs are the summarized main ideas of each of the subsequent three paragraphs.

Notice that in the last paragraph, finding the main idea is slightly more complex than just focusing on the first sentence. In fact the main idea of this paragraph is summarized by focusing on the second sentence and the final sentence of the paragraph.

Chapter 4
of
READING COMPREHENSION

THE SEVEN
STRATEGIES

In This Chapter . . .

QUESTION TYPES

As discussed earlier, GMAT Reading Comprehension questions come in a variety of forms, but they can be placed into 2 major categories:

1. GENERAL questions
2. SPECIFIC questions

In the following chapter, you will learn 7 strategies for answering Reading Comprehension questions. The first of these strategies will help you answer General questions. The second and third strategies will help you answer Specific questions. The last four strategies are applicable to both General and Specific questions.

General questions can often be answered without having to read the entire passage.

General Questions

General questions deal with the main idea, purpose, organization, and structure of a passage. Typical general questions are phrased as follows:

The primary purpose of the passage is
The main topic of the passage is
The author's primary objective in the passage is
Which of the following best describes the organization of the passage?
The passage as a whole can best be characterized as which of the following?

The correct answer to general questions such as *What is the main idea of this passage?* should relate to as much of the passage as possible.

Your Skeletal Sketch, and your understanding of the passage gained through generating the Skeletal Sketch, provide the keys to answering general questions. You should be able to answer general questions without having to re-read the entire passage. In fact, reading the entire passage can actually be distracting. At least one of the incorrect answer choices will usually pertain to a key detail contained in only one of the body paragraphs. If your initial reading focused on the structure of the passage and skimmed over the details, you will not be tempted to select these incorrect answer choices.

Occasionally, you may find yourself stuck between two answer choices on a general question. If this is the case, you should choose between answer choices by determining which answer choice relates to more paragraphs in the passage. Assign the answer choice 2 points if it relates to the first paragraph. If the answer choice relates to other paragraphs, assign it 1 point for each of these paragraphs. The answer choice with more points is usually the correct one. In the event of a tie, select the answer choice that pertains to the first paragraph over any choices that do not.

STRATEGY: If you are stuck between two answer choices, use a point system to assign a value to each one.

Specific Questions

Specific questions deal with details, inferences, assumptions, and arguments. Typical specific questions are phrased as follows:

> **According to the passage**
> **It can be inferred from the passage that**
> **All of the following statements are supported by the passage EXCEPT**
> **Which of the following is an assumption underlying the statement that**

In contrast to your approach to General questions, you will need to read the details in the passage to answer Specific questions. First, read the question focusing on the words in the question that you are most likely to find in the passage. Then, use your Headline List or Skeletal Sketch to identify the paragraph of the passage that most likely contains the information related to the key words from the question.

Use the structure provided by your Headline List or Skeletal Sketch to help decide which paragraph contains the correct answer.

> **STRATEGY: Identify the words in the question that you are most likely to find in the passage. Then, go back to the passage and find those key words.**

Consider the limbs of the sample Skeletal Sketch below:

> In reality, standardized tests have very little predictive validity
>
> Speeded test implies that being fast and being smart are the same, but this is not the case
>
> Tests are biased against non-native English speakers

If presented with the question: **Robinson raises the issue of cultural bias to do which of the following?**

you should use the limbs of your skeletal sketch, along with your scan of the passage, to decide that the key words in the question−**cultural bias**−will most likely be found in the last paragraph. Sometimes, you will need to find a synonym for the key words in the question. For example, if the question addresses **weapons of mass destruction**, you may need to find a paragraph that addresses **nuclear and chemical weapons**.

Once you identify the relevant paragraph, you should reread it to answer the question.

> **STRATEGY: You should be able to find ONE or TWO sentences in this paragraph to defend the correct answer choice.**

Only a small handful of GMAT questions require more than two sentences to defend the correct answer choice.

Strategies for All Reading Comprehension Questions

There are several question-attack strategies that you should implement for all Reading Comprehension passages. These include:

STRATEGY: JUSTIFY every word in the answer choice.

In the correct answer choice, every word should be completely true and within the scope of the passage. If you cannot justify *every* word in the answer choice, eliminate it. For example, consider the answer choices below:

(A) The colonists resented the king for taxing them without representation.

(B) England's policy of taxation without representation caused resentment among the colonists.

The difference in these two answer choices lies in the word **king** versus the word **England**. Although this seems like a small difference, it is the key to eliminating one of these answer choices. If the passage does not mention the king when it discusses the colonists' resentment, then the word **king** cannot be justified, and the answer choice should be eliminated.

One word can render an otherwise acceptable answer choice incorrect.

STRATEGY: AVOID extreme words.

Avoid Reading Comprehension answer choices that use extreme words. These words—such as **all**, **never, directly**, etc.—unnecessarily broaden the scope of an answer choice or make it too extreme. The GMAT always prefers moderate language and ideas. Eliminate answer choices that go too far.

STRATEGY: INFER as little as possible.

Many Reading Comprehension questions ask you to infer something from the passage. An inference is an informed deduction based on the information in the passage. Reading Comprehension inferences rarely go far beyond what is stated in the passage. In general, you should infer so little that the inference seems obvious. If an answer choice can be confirmed by language in the passage, this will almost always be the correct answer choice. Conversely, you should eliminate answer choices that require any logical stretch or leap from the passage.

> **STRATEGY: PREVIEW the first question.**

As you are reading through a passage for the first time and creating a Headline List or Skeletal Sketch, you will not know all of the questions which you will have to answer relating to that passage (as the questions appear on the computer screen one at a time). However, you will know the FIRST question, as this appears on the screen initially, together with the passage. It is important to read this question before reading the passage so that you can have one question in the back of your mind while you read and sketch. Most of the time, this first question will be a GENERAL question (e.g. **What is the purpose of the passage?**), but occasionally it will be a SPECIFIC question that focuses on a particular detail or section of the passage. Knowing the question before you read can help you to focus and save time later.

The first question on a reading passage is typically, though not always, a General question that can be answered by using your Headline List or Skeletal Sketch.

The Seven Strategies for Reading Comprehension

In summary, there are seven effective strategies you can use to answer Reading Comprehension questions on the GMAT. You may wish to jot these strategies down on your scratch paper before beginning the verbal section on test day. At the very least, you should commit them to memory and use them when you practice answering questions.

For GENERAL questions:

(1) Use a **POINT SYSTEM** when stuck between two answer choices.

For SPECIFIC questions:

(2) Match **KEY WORDS** in specific questions to key words (or synonyms) in the passage.

(3) **DEFEND** your answer choice with 1 to 2 sentences.

For ALL questions:

(4) **JUSTIFY** every word in your answer choice.

(5) Avoid answer choices that contain **EXTREME** words.

(6) Choose an answer choice that **INFERS** as **LITTLE** as possible.

And don't forget to:

(7) **PREVIEW** the first question before reading the passage.

Practice using the 7 strategies by answering Reading Comprehension questions found in *The Official Guide for GMAT Review.*

Chapter 5
of
READING COMPREHENSION

QUESTION
ANALYSIS

In This Chapter . . .

- Question Type Analysis
- **Insect Behavior** Passage & Headline List Revisited
- Four Questions & Explanations on **Insect Behavior**
- **Electroconvulsive Therapy** Passage & Skeletal Sketch Revisited
- Five Questions & Explanations on **Electroconvulsive Therapy**

QUESTION TYPE ANALYSIS

Answering GMAT Reading Comprehension questions is best learned by repeated practice with real GMAT reading passages and questions. You should spend a substantial amount of time with the passages found in *The Official Guide for GMAT Review, 11th Edition* and *The Official Guide for GMAT Verbal Review* to develop your familiarity with GMAT Reading Comprehension question types.

In this chapter, we will review two of the passages used as examples in the previous chapters covering Short and Long passages. Now, we will use the Headline List and Skeletal Sketch that we created for each passage in order to answer questions of the types you will see on the GMAT.

Note: For the purpose of practice and exposure to different question types, we will be reviewing four questions on the Short passage and five questions on the Long passage. However, on the GMAT, a short passage will typically have only 3 questions associated with it and a Long passage will typically have only 4 questions associated with it.

Please take the time to review the first passage, which is reproduced on the following page for your convenience. On the pages that follow, try answering each question in the appropriate amount of time (between 60 and 90 seconds) BEFORE you read the accompanying explanation.

The best way to familiarize yourself with the variety of Reading Comprehension question types is to answer real practice questions found in The Official Guide for GMAT Review.

Model Short Passage Revisited: *Insect Behavior*

Insect behavior generally appears to be explicable in terms of unconscious stimulus-response mechanisms; when scrutinized, it often reveals a stereotyped, inflexible quality. A classic example is the behavior of the female sphex wasp. In a typical case, the mother leaves her egg sealed in a burrow alongside a paralyzed grasshopper, which her larva can eat when it hatches. Before she deposits the grasshopper in the burrow, she leaves it at the entrance and goes inside to inspect the burrow. If the inspection reveals no problems, she drags the grasshopper inside by its antennae. Scientific experiments have uncovered an inability on the wasp's part to change its behavior when experiencing disruptions of this routine.

Charles Darwin discovered that if the grasshopper's antennae are removed the wasp will not drag it into the burrow, even though the legs or ovipositor could serve the same function as the antennae. Later Jean-Henri Fabre found more evidence of the wasp's dependence on predetermined routine. While a wasp was performing her inspection of a burrow, he moved the grasshopper a few centimeters away from the burrow's mouth. The wasp brought the grasshopper back to the edge of the burrow, then began a whole new inspection. When Fabre took this opportunity to move the food again, the wasp repeated her routine. Fabre performed his disruptive maneuver forty times, and the wasp's response never changed.

Review the model passage and Headline List and try to answer the questions that follow before reading the explanations.

Model Headline List for *Insect Behavior*

Insect behavior: displays unconscious stimulus-response mechanisms, inflexible quality
--(female sphex wasp)
--Experiments show inability to change routine

D: discovered wasp won't drag grasshopper if no antennae
Later, F: found more evidence of dependence upon routine

1. The primary purpose of the passage is to _____.

(A) prove, based on examples, that insects lack consciousness
(B) argue that insects are unique in their dependence on rigid routines
(C) analyze the maternal behavior of wasps
(D) compare and contrast the work of Darwin and Fabre
(E) argue that insect behavior relies on rigid routines which appear to be unconscious

This is a GENERAL question, so we should be able to answer the question based upon our understanding of the passage gained through creating our Headline List. For questions asking about the main idea of the passage, be sure to refer to the opening paragraph, which usually articulates the main idea.

We can eliminate **(A)** based upon the topic sentence in the first paragraph. The passage does not claim to prove that insects lack consciousness; it merely suggests, rather tentatively, that insect behavior "appears to be explicable" in terms of unconscious mechanisms. The language "lack consciousness" is too extreme in answer choice **(A)**.

Answer choice **(B)** reflects the language of the passage in that the passage does indicate that insects depend on rigid routines. However, it does not address the question of whether there are any other animals that depend on such routines, as is stated in answer choice **(B)**. The passage makes no claim about whether or not insects are "unique" in this respect. Remember that every word in an answer choice must be justified from the text.

We can eliminate answer choice **(C)** using our Headline List. It is clear that the sphex wasp is used as an example to illustrate a more general point, and is not itself the main point of the passage.

The fact that Fabre and Darwin only appear in the second paragraph is a good indication that they are not the passage's primary concern. Fabre and Darwin are simply mentioned as sources for some of the information on wasps. Answer choice **(D)** is incorrect.

(E) CORRECT. The passage begins with a topic sentence that announces the author's thesis. The thesis has two parts, as this answer choice correctly indicates: (i) insect behavior relies on rigid routines, and (ii) these routines appear to be unconscious. The topic sentence does not use the term "rigid routine", but it conveys the idea of rigidity by describing insect behavior as "inflexible"; the concept of routine is introduced later in the passage.

This correct answer choice is typical of the GMAT, in that it avoids restating word-for-word from the passage, instead using other synonymous terms (e.g. "rigid" instead of "inflexible").

The correct answer choice sometimes uses synonyms of key words contained in the passage to convey a particular idea using slightly different language.

2. The second paragraph performs which of the following functions in the passage?

(A) It provides experimental evidence of the inflexibility of one kind of insect behavior.
(B) It contradicts the conventional wisdom about "typical" wasp behavior.
(C) It illustrates the strength of the wasp's maternal affection.
(D) It explores the logical implications of the thesis articulated in the first paragraph.
(E) It highlights historical changes in the conduct of scientific research.

Questions that ask about the structure of a passage are GENERAL questions. We should be able to answer this type of question using our Headline List and our understanding of the organization of the passage.

Using our Headline List, we see that the main ideas of the second paragraph are:

D: discovered wasp won't drag grasshopper if no antennae
Later, F: found more evidence of dependence upon routine

Thus, the second paragraph describes experiments. Our Headline List indicates that the experiments are used as examples of inflexible insect behavior. This is mirrored closely in answer choice **(A)**, the correct answer.

We should always review all answer choices, as there may be more than one that seems promising.

Here, we can eliminate answer choice **(B)**. The passage does not mention any challenge to a conventional view; for all we know, the passage simply states the mainstream scientific position on insect behavior.

For answer choice **(C)** it might be tempting to infer that the wasp's persistence is caused by maternal affection. This inference is questionable, however, because the passage states that insect behavior is determined by mechanistic routines which appear to be unemotional in nature. Always avoid picking an answer choice that depends on a debatable inference, because the correct answer should not stray far from what is directly stated in the text.

Choice **(D)** is incorrect because Darwin's and Fabre's experiments do not explore the logical implications of the idea that insect behavior is inflexible. Rather, the experiments are presented as evidence of inflexibility.

Answer choice **(E)** goes beyond the scope of the passage. The paragraph mentions work by two scientists, but does not tell us whether any differences in their methods were part of a historical change in the conduct of science.

Even if one answer choice looks promising, always review all of the answer choices before making a selection.

*Manhattan*GMAT*Prep
the new standard

3. The passage mentions the grasshopper's ovipositor in the second paragraph in order to

(A) shed light on an anatomical peculiarity of grasshoppers
(B) illustrate the wasp's inability to avail itself of alternative methods
(C) provide a scientific synonym for the word "leg"
(D) invoke Darwin's theory of functional evolution
(E) concede that a grasshopper becomes difficult to move when its antennae are
    removed

You should be able to
justify every word in
the answer choice
that you select.

This is a SPECIFIC question that refers to a specific detail in the text of the passage. The first step in answering this question is to figure out where the word "ovipositor" occurs in the passage and re-read the surrounding sentence or sentences. This question is helpful in that it directs us to the second paragraph. We can quickly find the term "ovipositor" in the first sentence of that paragraph:

> **Charles Darwin discovered that if the grasshopper's antennae are removed the wasp will not drag it into the burrow, even though the legs or ovipositor could serve the same function as the antennae.**

We should use this sentence to justify the correct answer choice.

Answer choice **(A)** can be eliminated, as the sentence and the passage give us no anatomical information about grasshoppers, and do not tell us whether an ovipositor is a peculiarity of grasshoppers.

Answer choice **(B)** is related directly to the substance of our proof sentence. The ovipositor is mentioned as an alternative to the grasshopper's antennae that the wasp could have used in order to drag the grasshopper. Though this answer choice is a strong candidate for the correct choice, we should remember to review all answer choices, as sometimes more than one can seem correct, forcing us to distinguish between two answer choices more closely.

Answer choice **(C)** may be considered tempting. Perhaps the passage mentions the ovipositor as a technical term for a grasshopper leg. However, there are a number of clues that tell us "ovipositor" is not being presented as a synonym for *leg*:

(1) the passage reads "the legs [plural] or ovipositor", so we know "ovipositor" is not being presented as a synonym for "leg" (singular)
(2) the words "or ovipositor" are not set off with commas, as in "the leg, or ovipositor," which is the normal way of indicating that one word is a synonym for another
(3) "ovipositor" is a difficult word, and normally a passage will provide an easy synonym after a hard word, as in "the ovipositor, or leg," not the other way around.

Answer choice **(C)** is incorrect.

Answer choice **(D)** tries to tempt you by using assumed background knowledge. When you see the name "Darwin", you probably immediately think of Darwin's theory of evolution. On the GMAT, any answer choice that requires outside knowledge will generally be incorrect. The passage never mentions the theory of evolution, so we should eliminate answer choice **(D)**.

The words "even though the legs or ovipositor could serve the same function as the antennae" in our proof sentence indicate that using the legs or ovipositor would be no more difficult for the wasp than using the antennae to drag the grasshopper. We can eliminate answer choice **(E)** for this reason.

Thus, the correct answer to this problem is answer choice **(B)**.

Note: To answer this question, you do not need to know what "ovipositor" means; you just need to understand the logic of the sentence and the passage in which the word appears. But in case you are curious, an ovipositor is a tubular organ through which a female insect or fish deposits her eggs.

> **4. The passage supports which of the following statements about insect behavior?**
>
> (A) Reptiles such as snakes behave more flexibly than do insects.
> (B) Insects such as honeybees can always be expected to behave inflexibly.
> (C) Insect behavior indicates that insects do not feel pain.
> (D) Stimulus-response mechanisms in insects have evolved because, under ordinary circumstances, they help insects to survive.
> (E) There are many examples of insects other than wasps displaying inflexible, routine behaviors.

This is a SPECIFIC question that is quite difficult because many of the answer choices sound reasonable. The key to finding the correct answer is to focus on what is explicitly stated in the passage, and to examine whether each answer choice goes beyond what can be supported by the passage. Here, our Headline List and our understanding of the structure of the passage would direct us to the first paragraph. Again, you should be able to justify every word in the answer choice that you select.

Answer choice **(A)** mentions reptiles and snakes. Since the passage never mentions either of these, you should eliminate this answer choice. This is the case even though one could argue that the passage draws an implicit contrast between insect inflexibility and the more flexible behavior of some other creatures. You should discard any answer choice that goes too far beyond the passage.

Answer choice **(B)** is a great example of a tempting GMAT answer choice. Honeybees are insects, and the passage does claim that insect behavior tends to be inflexible. However, the passage does not say that every single species of insect behaves inflexibly; perhaps honeybees are an exception. Further, this answer choice states that honeybees *always* behave inflexibly, whereas the author states that insect behavior "*often* reveals a

Sidebar (left margin): The correct answer will NOT require the use of outside knowledge so eliminate any answer choice that does.

stereotyped, inflexible quality." "Always" is an extreme word, and cannot be justified in this answer choice.

Answer choice **(C)** requires us to infer that, because insects often display inflexible or unconscious behavior, they do not feel pain. Though one might associate these two attributes, there is nothing in the passage that indicates or even mentions the sensory perceptions of insects. Answer choice **(C)** goes too far beyond the passage.

The passage never explicitly mentions evolution, nor does it make any statement about why insects have stimulus-response mechanisms. Answer choice **(D)** also requires drawing inferences from beyond the text of the passage.

Be careful to stick closely to the language of the passage, and avoid any answer choices that go too far.

The first sentence of the passage tells us that "Insect behavior generally appears to be explicable in terms of unconscious stimulus-response mechanisms" and "often reveals a stereotyped, inflexible quality." The passage goes on to describe the case of sphex wasps as "a classic example." The passage thus clearly indicates that the case of sphex wasps is one of many different examples of the inflexible nature of insect behavior. Note that "many" can be justified by the passage in a way that a more extreme term such as "always" cannot be. Answer choice **(E)** is correct.

On the following page, please take the time to review a model Long passage and Skeletal Sketch provided in an earlier chapter and reproduced on the following page for your convenience.

Model Long Passage Revisited: *Electroconvulsive Therapy*

Review the model passage and Skeletal Sketch and try to answer the questions that follow *before* reading the explanations.

Electroconvulsive therapy (ECT) is a controversial psychiatric treatment involving the induction of a seizure in a patient by passing electricity through the brain. While beneficial effects of electrically induced seizures are evident and predictable in most patients, a unified mechanism of action has not yet been established and remains the subject of numerous investigations. ECT is extremely effective against severe depression, some acute psychotic states, and mania, though, like many medical procedures, it has its risks.

Since the inception of ECT in 1938, the public has held a strongly negative conception of the procedure. Initially, doctors employed unmodified ECT. Patients were rendered instantly unconscious by the electrical current, but the strength of the muscle contractions from uncontrolled motor seizures often led to compression fractures of the spine or damage to the teeth. In addition to the effect this physical trauma had on public sentiment, graphic examples of abuse in books and movies, such as Ken Kesey's *One Flew Over the Cuckoo's Nest*, portrayed ECT as punitive, cruel, overused, and violative of patients' legal rights.

Modern ECT is virtually unrecognizable from its earlier days. The treatment is modified by the muscle relaxant succinylcholine, which renders muscle contractions virtually nonexistent. Additionally, patients are given a general anesthetic. Thus, the patient is asleep and fully unaware during the procedure, and the only outward sign of a seizure may be the rhythmic movement of the patient's hand or foot. ECT is generally used in severely depressed patients for whom psychotherapy and medication prove ineffective. It may also be considered when there is an imminent risk of suicide, since antidepressants often take several weeks to work effectively. Exactly how ECT exerts its effects is not known, but repeated applications affect several neurotransmitters in the brain, including serotonin, norepinephrine, and dopamine.

ECT has proven effective, but it is not without controversy. Though decades-old studies showing brain cell death have been refuted in recent research, many patients do report loss of memory for events that occurred in the days, weeks or months surrounding the ECT. Some patients have also reported that their short-term memories continue to be affected for months after ECT, though some doctors argue that this may reflect the type of amnesia sometimes associated with severe depression.

Model Skeletal Sketch: *Electroconvulsive Therapy*

ECT: <u>controv psych. treatment, electr. into brain to induce seizure</u>
--beneficial effects, but no unified mechanism of action
--works for severe depress, some psych. states, mania; has risks

Since inception in 1938, public dislikes ECT

Modern ECT totally different, modified treatment

ECT effective, but controversial due to memory loss issues

> The correct answer to a *primary purpose* question should reflect the content of the majority of the paragraphs of the passage.

1. The passage is primarily concerned with

(A) defending a controversial medical practice
(B) explaining a controversial medical treatment
(C) arguing for further testing of a certain medical approach
(D) summarizing recent research concerning a particular medical procedure
(E) relating the public concern toward a particular medical therapy

This is a GENERAL question, and asks for the primary purpose of the passage (though the question is worded slightly differently). We should be able to answer this question relying only upon our Skeletal Sketch and our understanding of the passage.

The answer to a primary purpose question should encompass information found throughout the entire passage, and should reflect the main ideas that we have identified for each paragraph. The topic sentence of the first paragraph indicates that the passage is about electroconvulsive therapy (ECT), a controversial medical treatment. The remainder of the passage explains, in general terms, what ECT is used for and why it is considered controversial.

Answer choice **(A)** states that the passage explicitly defends ECT. The passage addresses ECT in an objective manner; the author neither defends nor argues against the continued use of ECT as a viable medical therapy. Answer choice **(A)** is incorrect. Note that one incorrect word is often enough to rule out an answer choice.

Answer choice **(B)** is correct. The primary purpose of the passage is to explain ECT. This includes briefly discussing both its purpose and the reasons why it has generated such controversy. This answer choice is reflected in our Skeletal Sketch.

We should continue to rule out other answer choices.

Answer choice **(C)** describes a need for further testing that is suggested but never mentioned in the passage.

Although recent research concerning a particular side effect of ECT is mentioned in the final paragraph, this is not the primary purpose of the passage. This answer choice is too specific for a primary purpose question. It does not relate to the content of the passage as a whole. Using the point system strategy, this answer choice would receive one point since it relates to the final paragraph. In contrast, the correct answer choice (B) would be assigned 5 points since it relates to the first paragraph (2 points) and each of the subsequent 3 paragraphs (1 point each). Answer choice **(D)** is incorrect.

Use the point system strategy to help identify the correct answer to General questions.

The passage does state that ECT is a controversial procedure that the public views in a negative manner; however, the passage only focuses on public concern over the procedure in the second paragraph. This answer choice is too specific for a primary purpose question, and does not encompass the majority of the passage. Using the point system strategy, this answer choice would receive only one point since it relates to only the second paragraph. Thus, answer choice **(E)** is also incorrect.

> **2. Which of the following is NOT cited in the passage as a current or historical criticism of ECT?**
>
> (A) ECT causes the death of brain cells.
> (B) ECT has been used to punish certain individuals.
> (C) Seizures during ECT cause bodily harm.
> (D) Short-term memory loss results from ECT.
> (E) The mechanism by which ECT works is not fully understood.

This is a SPECIFIC question that asks us which criticism of ECT is NOT cited in the passage. A methodical process of elimination is the best approach to answer a "NOT" or "EXCEPT" question. Use your Skeletal Sketch and your understanding of the passage to quickly and accurately locate the important information in the passage, and then eliminate each answer choice as soon as you prove that it *is* cited as a criticism of ECT.

The final sentence of the second paragraph indicates that one of the reasons the public has a negative perception of ECT is that ECT has been portrayed as "punitive"; in other words, that ECT has been used to punish certain individuals. Thus, answer choice **(B)** can be eliminated.

The second paragraph explicitly and prominently mentions the bodily harm caused by seizures during unmodified ECT in its second and third sentences. Answer choice **(C)** is clearly incorrect.

The second sentence of the final paragraph indicates that the death of brain cells was the basis for an historical criticism of ECT. Although the research was recently refuted, brain cell death is still a side-effect that, at one time, caused criticism of the procedure. Answer choice **(A)** can be ruled out.

The second sentence of the final paragraph also cites short-term memory loss as the primary reason that ECT, in its current modified form, still generates controversy. Thus, answer choice **(D)** is incorrect.

Both the first and third paragraphs specifically state that the mechanism by which ECT works is not fully understood. However, these statements are offered in a neutral way, not as a criticism of ECT, but simply as additional information about the procedure. Answer choice **(E)** is the only answer choice that is not cited as a past or current criticism of ECT, and is the correct answer.

Note that, with this type of negative question, it is often easier to eliminate incorrect answer choices than to identify the correct answer choice.

Tone questions are General questions, but they often require a second look at the specific word choices in the passage.

3. The tone of the passage suggests that the author regards ECT with

    (A) conditional support
    (B) academic objectivity
    (C) mild advocacy
    (D) unreserved criticism
    (E) burgeoning acceptance

A tone question is an example of a GENERAL question. Though a tone question is often answerable using only one's Skeletal Sketch and understanding of the passage, it is often necessary to closely examine the specific words the author uses to convey information. Here, the author presents evidence both for and against the efficacy and safety of ECT, and does not clearly lean toward or against more widespread adoption of the treatment. When presenting criticisms of ECT, the author does so in a manner that does not indicate a clear bias or direction. The correct answer will reflect this balance.

Answer choice **(A)** is incorrect, as the author's tone does not indicate support for ECT. Moreover, there are no clear conditions placed upon any support by the author.

Answer choice **(B)** is the correct answer. The tone of the passage is impartial and objective. The passage explains the history and discussion of ECT in an unbiased, academic manner. We should still continue to examine all answer choices.

Answer choice **(C)** is incorrect, as the tone of the passage does not suggest even mild advocacy on the part of the author. Though the author admits the "proven" efficacy of ECT, this is more than counterbalanced by accounts of criticisms and controversy surrounding the treatment. The tone of the passage is not supportive overall.

Answer choice **(D)** is incorrect, as the language is too extreme. The tone of the passage is not unreserved, and the author is not clearly critical in his stance toward ECT.

Answer choice **(E)** is also not an accurate representation of the tone of the passage. It may be the case that ECT has achieved growing acceptance since its inception, but this reflects the popular or medical perception, not that of the author.

4. Which of the following can be inferred from the third paragraph?

(A) Greater amounts of the neurotransmitters serotonin, norepinephrine, and dopamine seem to reduce symptoms of depression.
(B) ECT is never used prior to attempting psychotherapy or medication.
(C) Succinylcholine completely immobilizes the patient's entire body.
(D) ECT often takes fewer than several weeks to work effectively.
(E) One ECT treatment is often sufficient to significantly reduce symptoms of depression.

> Even though an inference is not directly stated in the passage, you should still be able to defend it using one or two sentences from the passage.

This is an inference question, which is a SPECIFIC question. The answer to an inference question must be directly supported by evidence from the text. As always, be sure to pay particular attention to the precise words used in the answer choices and how they relate to the information presented in the passage.

For answer choice **(A)**, the third paragraph specifically states that ECT "affects" these particular neurotransmitters. However, no information is provided to suggest how these neurotransmitters are affected. Since the passage does not indicate an increase in these neurotransmitters, this cannot be the best answer.

The third paragraph states that "ECT is generally used in severely depressed patients for whom psychotherapy and medication prove ineffective." This does not mean that ECT is "never" used before these other therapies. Answer choice **(B)** is too extreme to be the correct answer for this inference question.

According to the third paragraph, succinylcholine renders muscle contractions "virtually nonexistent," rather than "completely" nonexistent. Moreover, the passage states that a patient's hand or foot may rhythmically move during ECT. Thus the patient's entire body is not completely immobilized. Eliminate answer choice **(C)**.

The paragraph also states that ECT may be used "when there is an imminent risk of suicide, since antidepressants often take several weeks to work effectively." The conjunction "since" indicates that the length of time ECT takes to work is being contrasted with that of antidepressants. Additionally, the phrase "imminent risk" suggests a swift solution is necessary. Thus, ECT must in some cases work in fewer than several weeks. We see that this choice can be justified directly from proof sentences from the passage. Answer choice **(D)** is correct.

The final sentence of the third paragraph states that "repeated applications" of ECT affect several neurotransmitters. This suggests that patients undergo several ECT applications during the course of treatment. Answer choice **(E)** is incorrect.

5. According to the passage, which of the following statements is true?

(A) Most severely depressed individuals have suicidal thoughts.
(B) The general public was unaware of the bodily harm caused by unmodified ECT.
(C) Research into the side-effects of ECT has only recently begun.
(D) ECT does not benefit individuals with anxiety disorders.
(E) Severe depression can have symptoms unrelated to mood.

This is a difficult SPECIFIC question that does not indicate a particular part of the passage. As with a "NOT" or "EXCEPT" question, a methodical process of elimination is helpful in answering a question that does not provide a particular key word or phrase. Use your Skeletal sketch to quickly and accurately locate the important information in the passage, and then eliminate each answer choice as soon as you prove that it is not cited in the passage as true.

If a passage is silent about a particular point, this does not mean that the point is necessarily untrue.

The third paragraph of the passage indicates that ECT is considered as a treatment option "when there is an imminent risk of suicide." However, nothing in the passage suggests the percentage (or number) of severely depressed individuals who have suicidal thoughts. Answer choice **(A)** can be eliminated.

The second paragraph of the passage states that the public was well aware of the bodily harm caused by unmodified ECT. This knowledge influenced the general public's "strongly negative conception of the procedure." Answer choice **(B)** is incorrect.

The second sentence of the final paragraph cites "decades-old studies" of ECT. Thus, research has not recently begun. Answer choice **(C)** should be ruled out.

The first paragraph states that "ECT is extremely effective against severe depression, some acute psychotic states, and mania." This does NOT necessarily mean that ECT is ineffective for anxiety disorders. With an "according to the passage" question, the correct answer must be provable by the passage text. Answer choice **(D)** is not shown by the passage to be true.

The final sentence of the passage states that amnesia is a possible side-effect of severe depression. Amnesia is a memory disorder and is clearly not related to mood. Answer choice **(E)** is correct.

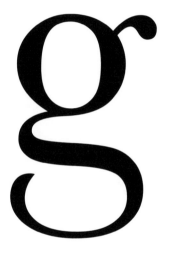

Chapter 6
of
READING COMPREHENSION

PASSAGES &
PROBLEM SETS

Problem Set

The following problem set consists of reading passages followed by a series of questions on each passage. Use the following guidelines as you complete this problem set:

1) Before you read each passage, identify whether it is LONG or SHORT.

2) Preview the first question before reading, but do not look at any of the subsequent questions prior to reading the passage, since you will not be able to do this on the GMAT.

3) As you read the passage, create a Headline List (for SHORT passages) or a Skeletal Sketch (for LONG passages). Then, use your Headline List or Skeletal Sketch to assist you in answering all the questions that accompany the passage.

4) Before answering each question, identify it as either a General question or a Specific question. Use the 7 strategies for Reading Comprehension to assist you in answering the questions.

5) On the GMAT, you will typically see 3 questions on SHORT passages and 4 questions on LONG passages. However, in this problem set, you will see 5 questions associated with each passage. As such, use the following MODIFIED timing guidelines:

For Short Passages: Spend approximately 2 to 3 minutes reading and creating your Headline List. Spend approximately 60 seconds answering General questions and between 60 to 90 seconds answering Specific questions. Do not spend more than 9 minutes in total reading, writing, and answering all the questions on a Short passage. (Keep in mind that on the real GMAT, when you only see 3 questions on a typical Short passage, you should finish in approximately 6 minutes.)

For Long Passages: Spend approximately 3 minutes reading and creating your Skeletal Sketch. Spend approximately 60 seconds answering General questions and between 60 to 90 seconds answering Specific questions. Do not spend more than 9 minutes in total reading, writing, and answering all the questions on a Long passage. (Keep in mind that on the real GMAT, when you only see 4 questions on a typical Long passage, you should finish in approximately 8 minutes.)

Passage A: Japanese Swords

Historians have long recognized the Japanese sword as one of the finest cutting weapons ever created. But to consider the sword that is synonymous with the samurai as merely a weapon is to ignore what makes it so special. The Japanese sword has always been considered a splendid weapon and even a spiritual entity. The traditional Japanese saying "The sword is the soul of the samurai" not only reflects the sword's importance to its wielder but also is indicative of its importance to its creator, the master smith.

Master smiths may not have been considered artists in the classical sense, but every one of them took great care in how he created a sword, and no sword was created in exactly the same way. The forging process of the blade itself took hundreds of hours as two types of steel were heated, hammered and folded together many times. This created a blade consisting of thousands of very thin layers that had an extremely sharp and durable cutting edge; at the same time, the blade was flexible and therefore less likely to break. It was common, though optional, for a master smith to place a physical signature on a blade; in addition, every master smith had a "structural signature" due to his own secret forging process. Each master smith brought a high level of devotion, skill, and attention to detail to the sword-making process, and the sword itself was a reflection of his personal honor and ability. This effort made each blade as unique as the samurai who wielded it; today the Japanese sword is recognized as much for its artistic merit as its historical significance.

1. The primary purpose of the passage is to

(A) challenge the observation that the Japanese sword is highly admired by historians
(B) introduce new information about the forging of Japanese swords
(C) identify how the Japanese sword is now perceived as much for its artistic qualities as its military ones
(D) argue that Japanese sword makers were as much artists as they were smiths
(E) explain the value attributed to the Japanese sword

2. Each of the following is mentioned in the passage EXCEPT

(A) Every Japanese sword has a unique structure that can be traced back to a special forging process.
(B) Master smiths kept their forging techniques secret.

(C) The Japanese sword was considered by some to have a spiritual quality.

(D) Master smiths are now considered artists by most major historians.

(E) The Japanese sword is now considered as much a work of art as it is a weapon.

3. The author is most likely to agree with which of the following observations?

(A) The Japanese sword is the most important handheld weapon in history.

(B) The skill of the samurai is what made the Japanese sword so special.

(C) If a sword had a physical signature, other swords could be attributed to that sword's creator.

(D) Master smiths were more concerned about the artistic merit of their blades than about the blades' practical qualities.

(E) The Japanese sword has more historical importance than artistic importance.

4. Which of the following can be inferred about the term "structural signature" in this passage?

(A) It indicates the inscription that the smith places on the blade during the forging process.

(B) It implies the particular characteristics of a blade created by a smith's unique forging process.

(C) It suggests that each blade can be traced back to a known master smith.

(D) It demonstrates the effort and attention that each master smith devoted to the creation of swords.

(E) It refers to the actual curved shape of the blade.

5. One function of the second paragraph of the passage is to

(A) present an explanation for a change in perception

(B) determine the historical significance of Japanese swords

(C) explain why each Japanese sword is unique

(D) compare Japanese master smiths to classical artists

(E) review the complete process of making a Japanese sword

Passage B: Television's Invention

In the early years of television, Vladimir Zworykin was, at least in the public sphere, recognized as its inventor. His loudest champion was his boss, David Sarnoff, then president of RCA and a man that we regard even today as "the father of television." Current historians agree that Philo Farnsworth, a self-educated prodigy who was the first to transmit live images, was television's true inventor.

In his own time, Farnsworth's contributions went largely unnoticed, in large part because he was excluded from the process of introducing the invention to a national audience. Sarnoff put televisions into living rooms, and Sarnoff was responsible for a dominant paradigm of the television industry that continues to be relevant today: advertisers pay for the programming so that they can have a receptive audience for their products. Sarnoff had already utilized this construct to develop the radio industry, and it had, within ten years, become ubiquitous. Farnsworth thought the television should be used as an educational tool, but he had little understanding of the business world, and was never able to implement his ideas.

Perhaps one can argue that Sarnoff simply adapted the business model for radio and television from the newspaper industry, replacing the revenue from subscriptions and purchases of individual newspapers with that of selling the television sets themselves, but Sarnoff promoted himself as nothing less than a visionary. Some television critics argue that the construct Sarnoff implemented has played a negative role in determining the content of the programs themselves, while others contend that it merely created a democratic platform from which the audience can determine the types of programming it wants.

1. The primary purpose of the passage is to

(A) correct public misconception about Farnsworth's role in developing early television programs
(B) debate the influence of television on popular culture
(C) challenge the current public perception of Vladimir Zworykin
(D) chronicle the events that led up to the invention of the television
(E) describe Sarnoff's influence on the public perception of television's inception, and debate the impact of Sarnoff's paradigm

2. It can be inferred from the third paragraph of the passage that

ManhattanGMAT Prep
the new standard

(A) television shows produced by David Sarnoff and Vladimir Zworykin tended to earn negative reviews
(B) educational programs cannot draw as large an audience as sports programs
(C) a number of critics feel that Sarnoff's initial decision to earn television revenue through advertising has had a positive or neutral impact on content
(D) educational programs that are aired in prime time, the hours during which the greatest number of viewers are watching television, are less likely to earn a profit than those that are aired during the daytime hours
(E) in matters of programming, the audience's preferences should be more influential than those of the advertisers

3. **Which of the following best illustrates the relationship between the second and third paragraphs?**

(A) The second paragraph dissects the evolution of a contemporary controversy; the third paragraph presents differing viewpoints on that controversy.
(B) The second paragraph explores the antithetical intentions of two men involved in the infancy of an industry; the third paragraph details the eventual deterioration of that industry.
(C) The second paragraph presents differing views of a historical event; the third paragraph represents the author's personal opinion about that event.
(D) The second paragraph provides details that are necessary to support the author's opinion, which is presented in the third paragraph.
(E) The second paragraph presents divergent visions about the possible uses of a technological device; the third paragraph initiates a debate about the ramifications of one of those perspectives.

4. **According to the passage, the television industry, at its inception, earned revenue from**

(A) advertising only
(B) advertising and the sale of television sets
(C) advertising and subscriptions
(D) subscriptions and the sale of television sets
(E) advertising, subscriptions, and the sale of television sets

5. **The passage suggests that Farnsworth might have earned greater public notoriety for his invention if**

(A) Vladimir Zworykin had been less vocal about his own contributions to the television
(B) Farnsworth had been able to develop and air his own educational programs
(C) Farnsworth had involved Sarnoff in his plans to develop, manufacture, or distribute the television
(D) Sarnoff had involved Farnsworth in his plans to develop, manufacture, or distribute the television
(E) Farnsworth had a better understanding of the type of programming the audience wanted to watch most

*Manhattan*GMAT°Prep

Passage C: Life on Mars

Because of the proximity and likeness of Mars to Earth, scientists have long speculated about the possibility of life on Mars. As early as the mid-17th century, astronomers observed polar ice caps on Mars, and by the mid-19th century, scientists discovered other similarities to Earth, including the length of day and axial tilt. But in 1965, photos taken by the Mariner 4 probe revealed a Mars without rivers, oceans or signs of life. And in the 1990s, it was discovered that Mars, unlike Earth, no longer possessed a substantial global magnetic field, allowing celestial radiation to reach the planet's surface and solar wind to eliminate much of Mars's atmosphere over the course of several billion years.

More recent probes have focused on whether there was once water on Mars. Some scientists believe that this question is definitively answered by the presence of certain geological landforms. Others posit that different explanations, such as wind erosion or carbon dioxide oceans, may be responsible for these formations. Mars rovers Opportunity and Spirit, which have been exploring the surface of Mars since 2004, have both discovered geological evidence of past water activity. These findings substantially bolster claims that there was once life on Mars.

1. **The author's stance on the possibility of life on Mars can best be described as**

(A) optimistic
(B) disinterested
(C) skeptical
(D) simplistic
(E) cynical

2. **The passage is primarily concerned with which of the following?**

(A) disproving a widely accepted theory
(B) initiating a debate about the possibility of life on Mars
(C) presenting evidence in support of a controversial claim
(D) describing the various discoveries made concerning the possibility of life on Mars
(E) detailing the findings of the Mars rovers Opportunity and Spirit

3. **Each of the following discoveries is mentioned in the passage EXCEPT**

(A) Wind erosion and carbon dioxide oceans are responsible for certain geological landforms on Mars.

*Manhattan*GMAT®Prep
the new standard

(B) Mars does not have a substantial global magnetic field.
(C) Mars does not currently have water activity.
(D) The length of day on Mars is similar to that on Earth.
(E) The axial tilt of Mars is similar to that of Earth.

4. **In the first paragraph, the author most likely mentions the discovery of polar ice caps to suggest that**

(A) until recently Mars' polar ice caps were thought to consist largely of carbon dioxide
(B) Martian polar ice caps are made almost entirely of water ice
(C) Mars has many similarities to Earth, including the existence of polar ice caps
(D) Mars has only a small fraction of the carbon dioxide found on Earth and Venus
(E) conditions on the planet Mars were once very different than they are at present

5. **Each of the following can be inferred from the passage EXCEPT**

(A) The presence of certain geological landforms is not definitive proof that there was once life on Mars.
(B) It is likely that there were few significant discoveries related to the possibility of life on Mars prior to the mid-17th century.
(C) The absence of a substantial global magnetic field on Mars suggests that it would be difficult to sustain life on Mars.
(D) The presence of water activity on Mars is related to the possibility of life on Mars.
(E) The claim that there was once water on Mars has only limited and indirect support from recent discoveries.

Passage D: Fossils

In archaeology, as with the physical sciences, new discoveries frequently undermine accepted findings and give rise to new theories. This can be seen in the reaction to the recent discovery of a set of 3.3-million-year-old fossils in Ethiopia that comprise the earliest well-preserved child ever found. The fossilized child was estimated to be about 3 years old at death, female, and a member of the Australopithecus afarensis species. The afarensis species, a major human ancestor, lived in Africa from earlier than 3.7 million to 3 million years ago. "Her completeness, antiquity and age at death make this find of unprecedented importance in the history of paleo-anthropology," said Zeresenay Alemseged, a noted paleo-anthropologist. Other scientists said that the discovery could reconfigure conceptions about the lives and capacities of these early humans.

Prior to this discovery, it had been thought that the afarensis species had abandoned the arboreal habitat of their ape cousins. However, while the lower limbs of this fossil supported findings that afarensis walked upright, its gorilla-like arms and shoulders suggested that it retained the ability to swing through trees. This has initiated a reexamination of many accepted theories of early human development. Also, the presence of a hyoid bone, a rarely preserved bone in the larynx that supports muscles of the throat, has had a tremendous impact on theories about the origins of speech. The fossil bone is primitive and more similar to those of apes than humans, but it is the first hyoid found in such an early human-related species.

1. **The organization of the passage could best be described as**

(A) discussing a controversial scientific discovery
(B) contrasting previous theories of development with current findings
(C) illustrating a contention with a specific example
(D) arguing the importance of a particular field of study
(E) refuting a popular misconception

2. **The passage quotes Zeresenay Alemseged in order to**

(A) provide evidence to support the main idea of the first paragraph
(B) question the claims of other scientists
(C) provide evidence to support the linguistic abilities of the afarensis species

(D) provide evidence that supports the significance of the find
(E) provide a subjective opinion that is refuted in the second paragraph

3. **Each of the following is cited as a factor in the importance of the discovery of the fossils EXCEPT**

(A) the fact that the remains were those of a child
(B) the age of the fossils
(C) the location of the discovery
(D) the species of the fossils
(E) the intact nature of the fossils

4. **It can be inferred from the passage's description of the discovered fossil hyoid bone that**

(A) Australopithecus afarensis were capable of speech
(B) the discovered hyoid bone is less primitive than the hyoid bone of apes
(C) the hyoid bone is necessary for speech
(D) the discovery of the hyoid bone necessitated the reexamination of prior theories
(E) the hyoid bone was the most important fossil found at the site

5. **According to the passage, the impact of the discovery of the hyoid bone in the field of archaeology could best be compared to which one of the following examples in another field?**

(A) The discovery and analysis of cosmic rays lend support to a widely accepted theory of the origin of the universe.
(B) The original manuscript of a deceased 19th century author confirms ideas of the development of an important work of literature.
(C) The continued prosperity of a state-run economy stirs debate in the discipline of macroeconomics.
(D) Newly revealed journal entries by a prominent Civil War era politician lead to a questioning of certain accepted historical interpretations about the conflict.
(E) Research into the mapping of the human genome gives rise to nascent applications of individually tailored medicines.

Passage E: Polygamy

Polygamy in Africa has been a popular topic for social research over the past four decades; it has been analyzed by many distinguished minds and in various well-publicized works. In 1961, when Remi Clignet published his book "Many Wives, Many Powers," he was not alone in sharing the view that in Africa co-wives may be perceived as direct and indirect sources of increased income and prestige.

By the 1970s, such arguments had become crystallized and popular. Many other African scholars who wrote on the subject became the new champions of this philosophy. For example, in 1983, John Mbiti proclaimed that polygamy is an accepted and respectable institution serving many useful social purposes. Similarly, G.K. Nukunya, in his paper "Polygamy as a Symbol of Status," reiterated Mbiti's idea that a plurality of wives is a sign of affluence and power in the African society.

However, the colonial missionary voice provided one consistent opposition to polygamy by viewing the practice as unethical and destructive of family life. While they propagated this view with the authority of the Bible, they were convinced that Africans had to be coerced into partaking in the vision of monogamy understood by the Western culture. The missionary viewpoint even included, in some instances, dictating immediate divorce in the case of newly converted men who had already contracted polygamous marriages. Unfortunately, both the missionary voice and the scholarly voice did not consider the views of African women on the matter important. Although there was some awareness that women regarded polygamy as both a curse and a blessing, the distanced, albeit scientific, perspective of an outside observer predominated both on the pulpit and in scholarly writings.

Contemporary research in the social sciences has begun to focus on the protagonist's voice in the study of culture, recognizing that the views and experiences of those who take part in a given reality ought to receive close examination. This privileging of the protagonist seems appropriate, particularly given that women in Africa have often used literary productions to comment on marriage, family and gender relations.

1. Which of the following best describes the main purpose of the passage above?

(A) to discuss scholarly works that view polygamy as a sign of prestige, respect, and affluence in the African society

(B) to trace the origins of the missionary opposition to African polygamy

(C) to argue for imposing restrictions on polygamy in the African society
(D) to explore the reasons for women's acceptance of polygamy
(E) to discuss multiple perspectives on African polygamy and contrast them with contemporary research

2. **The third paragraph of the passage plays which of the following roles?**

(A) discusses the rationale for viewing polygamy as an indication of prestige and affluence in the African society
(B) supports the author's view that polygamy is unethical and destructive of family life
(C) contrasts the views of the colonial missionary with the position of the most recent contemporary research
(D) describes the views on polygamy held by the colonial missionary and indicates a flaw in this vision
(E) demonstrates that the colonial missionary was ignorant of the scholarly research on monogamy

3. **The passage provides each of the following, EXCEPT**

(A) the year of publication of Remi Clignet's book "Many Wives, Many Powers"
(B) the year in which John Mbiti made a claim that polygamy is an accepted institution
(C) examples of African women's literary productions devoted to family relations
(D) reasons for missionary opposition to polygamy
(E) current research perspectives on polygamy

4. **According to the passage, the colonial missionary and the early scholarly research shared which of the following traits in their views on polygamy?**

(A) both considered polygamy a sign of social status and success
(B) neither accounted for the views of local women
(C) both attempted to limit the prevalence of polygamy
(D) both pointed out polygamy's destructive effects on family life
(E) both exhibited a somewhat negative attitude towards polygamy

5. **Which of the following statements can most confidently be inferred from the passage?**

(A) Nukunya's paper "Polygamy as a Symbol of Status" was not written in 1981.
(B) John Mbiti adjusted his initial view on polygamy, recognizing that the experiences of African women should receive closer attention.
(C) Remi Clignet's book "Many Wives, Many Powers" was the first well-known scholarly work to proclaim that polygamy can be viewed as a symbol or prestige and wealth.
(D) Under the influence of the missionary opposition, polygamy was proclaimed illegal in Africa as a practice "unethical and destructive of family life."
(E) A large proportion of the scholars writing on polygamy in the 1970s and 1980s were of African descent.

*Manhattan*GMAT*Prep

Passage F: Sweet Spot

Though most tennis players generally strive to strike the ball on the racket's vibration node, more commonly known as the "sweet spot," many players are unaware of the existence of a second, lesser-known location on the racket face, the center of percussion, that will also greatly diminish the strain on a player's arm when the ball is struck.

In order to understand the physics of this second sweet spot, it is helpful to consider what would happen to a tennis racket in the moments after impact with the ball if the player's hand were to vanish at the moment of impact. The impact of the ball would cause the racket to bounce backwards, experiencing a translational motion away from the ball. The tendency of this motion would be to jerk all parts of the racket, including the end of its handle, backward, or away from the ball. Unless the ball happened to hit the racket precisely at the racket's center of mass, the racket would additionally experience a rotational motion around its center of mass – much as a penny that has been struck near its edge will start to spin. The effect of this rotational motion would be to jerk the end of the handle forward, towards the ball. Depending on where the ball struck the racket face, one or the other of these motions would predominate.

However, there is one point of impact, known as the center of percussion, which causes neither motion to predominate; if a ball were to strike this point, the impact would not impart any motion to the end of the handle. The reason for this lack of motion is that the force on the upper part of the hand would be equal and opposite to the force on the lower part of the hand, resulting in no net force on the tennis players' hand or forearm. The center of percussion constitutes a second sweet spot because a tennis player's wrist typically is placed next to the end of the racket's handle. When the player strikes the ball at the center of percussion, her wrist is jerked neither forward nor backward, and she experiences a relatively smooth, comfortable tennis stroke.

The manner in which a tennis player can detect the center of percussion on a given tennis racket follows from the nature of this second sweet spot. The center of percussion can be located via simple trial and error by holding the end of a tennis racket between your finger and thumb and throwing a ball onto the strings. If the handle jumps out of your hand, then the ball missed the center of percussion.

1. **What is the primary message the author is trying to convey?**

    (A) a proposal for an improvement to the design of tennis rackets
    (B) an examination of the differences between the two types of sweet spot
    (C) a definition of the translational and rotational forces acting on a tennis racket
    (D) a description of the ideal area in which to strike every ball
    (E) an explanation of a lesser-known area on a tennis racket that dampens unwanted vibration

2. **According to the passage, all of the following are true of the forces acting upon a tennis racket striking a ball EXCEPT**

    (A) The only way to eliminate the jolt that accompanies most strokes is to hit the ball on the center of percussion.
    (B) The impact of the ball striking the racket can strain a tennis player's arm.
    (C) There are at least two different forces acting upon the racket.
    (D) The end of the handle of the racket will jerk forward after striking the ball unless the ball strikes the racket's center of mass.
    (E) The racket will rebound after it strikes the ball.

3. **What is the primary function served by paragraph two in the context of the entire passage?**

    (A) to establish the main idea of the passage
    (B) to provide an explanation of the mechanics of the phenomenon discussed in the passage
    (C) to introduce a counterargument that elucidates the main idea of the passage
    (D) to provide an example of the primary subject described in the passage
    (E) to explain why the main idea of the passage would be useful for tennis players

4. **The author mentions "a penny that has been struck near its edge" in order to**

    (A) show how the center of mass causes the racket to spin
    (B) argue that a penny spins in the exact way that a tennis racket spins
    (C) explain how translational motion works
    (D) provide an illustration of a concept
    (E) demonstrate that pennies and tennis rackets do not spin in the same way

5. **Which of the following can be inferred from the passage?**

    (A) If a player holds the tennis racket anywhere other than the end of the handle, the player will experience a jolting sensation.
    (B) The primary sweet spot is more effective at damping vibration than the secondary sweet spot.
    (C) Striking a tennis ball at a spot other than the center of percussion can result in a jarring feeling.
    (D) Striking a tennis ball repeatedly at spots other than a sweet spot leads to "tennis elbow."
    (E) If a player lets go of the racket at the moment of impact, the simultaneous forward and backward impetus causes the racket to drop straight to the ground.

Passage G: Chaos Theory

Around 1960, mathematician Edward Lorenz found unexpected behavior in apparently simple equations representing atmospheric air flows. Whenever he reran his model with the same inputs, different outputs resulted – although the model lacked any random elements. Lorenz realized that tiny rounding errors in his analog computer mushroomed over time, leading to erratic results. His findings marked a seminal moment in the development of chaos theory, which, despite its name, has little to do with randomness.

To understand how unpredictability can arise from deterministic equations, which do not involve chance outcomes, consider the non-chaotic system of two poppy seeds placed in a round bowl. As the seeds roll to the bowl's center, a position known as a point attractor, the distance between the seeds shrinks. If, instead, the bowl is flipped over, two seeds placed on top will roll away from each other. Such a system, while still not technically chaotic, enlarges initial differences in position.

Chaotic systems, such as a machine mixing bread dough, are characterized by both attraction and repulsion. As the dough is stretched, folded and pressed back together, any poppy seeds sprinkled in are intermixed seemingly at random. But this randomness is illusory. In fact, the poppy seeds are captured by "strange attractors," staggeringly complex pathways whose tangles appear accidental but are in fact determined by the system's fundamental equations.

During the dough-kneading process, two poppy seeds positioned next to each other eventually go their separate ways. Any early divergence or measurement error is repeatedly amplified by the mixing until the position of any seed becomes effectively unpredictable. It is this "sensitive dependence on initial conditions" and not true randomness that generates unpredictability in chaotic systems, of which one example may be the Earth's weather. According to the popular interpretation of the "Butterfly Effect," a butterfly flapping its wings causes hurricanes. A better understanding is that the butterfly causes uncertainty about the precise state of the air. This microscopic uncertainty grows until it encompasses even hurricanes. Few meteorologists believe that we will ever be able to predict rain or shine for a particular day years in the future.

1. The main purpose of this passage is to

(A) explain complicated aspects of certain physical systems
(B) trace the historical development of a scientific theory
(C) distinguish a mathematical pattern from its opposite
(D) describe the spread of a technical model from one field of study to others
(E) contrast possible causes of weather phenomena

2. In the example discussed in the passage, what is true about poppy seeds in bread dough, once the dough has been thoroughly mixed?

(A) They have been individually stretched and folded over, like miniature versions of the entire dough.
(B) They are scattered in random clumps throughout the dough.
(C) They are accidentally caught in tangled objects called strange attractors.
(D) They are bound to regularly dispersed patterns of point attractors.
(E) They are in positions dictated by the underlying equations that govern the mixing process.

3. According to the passage, the rounding errors in Lorenz's model

(A) indicated that the model was programmed in a fundamentally faulty way
(B) were deliberately included to represent tiny fluctuations in atmospheric air currents
(C) were imperceptibly small at first, but tended to grow
(D) were at least partially expected, given the complexity of the actual atmosphere
(E) shrank to insignificant levels during each trial of the model

4. The passage mentions each of the following as an example or potential example of a chaotic or non-chaotic system EXCEPT

(A) a dough-mixing machine
(B) atmospheric weather patterns
(C) poppy seeds placed on top of an upside-down bowl
(D) poppy seeds placed in a right-side-up bowl
(E) fluctuating butterfly flight patterns

5. It can be inferred from the passage that which of the following pairs of items would most likely follow typical pathways within a chaotic system?

(A) two particles ejected in random directions from the same decaying atomic nucleus
(B) two stickers affixed to a balloon that expands and contracts over and over again
(C) two avalanches sliding down opposite sides of the same mountain
(D) two baseballs placed into an active tumble dryer
(E) two coins flipped into a large bowl

**Answers to Passage A: Japanese Swords**

Historians have long recognized the Japanese sword as one of the finest cutting weapons ever created. But to consider the sword that is synonymous with the samurai as merely a weapon is to ignore what makes it so special. The Japanese sword has always been considered a splendid weapon and even a spiritual entity. The traditional Japanese saying "The sword is the soul of the samurai" not only reflects the sword's importance to its wielder but also is indicative of its importance to its creator, the master smith.

Master smiths may not have been considered artists in the classical sense, but every one of them took great care in how he created a sword, and no sword was created in exactly the same way. The forging process of the blade itself took hundreds of hours as two types of steel were heated, hammered and folded together many times. This created a blade consisting of thousands of very thin layers that had an extremely sharp and durable cutting edge; at the same time, the blade was flexible and therefore less likely to break. It was common, though optional, for a master smith to place a physical signature on a blade; in addition, every master smith had a "structural signature" due to his own secret forging process. Each master smith brought a high level of devotion, skill, and attention to detail to the sword-making process, and the sword itself was a reflection of his personal honor and ability. This effort made each blade as unique as the samurai who wielded it; today the Japanese sword is recognized as much for its artistic merit as its historical significance.

This is a SHORT passage (35 lines or fewer on page). Here is a model Headline List:

H: Long recognized J sword as one of best cutting weapons but it is more than just this that makes it special
--spiritual entity
--important to both wielder and creator, master smith

Master smiths took great care with swords and all swords are unique
--(forging process)
--(physical signature, structural signature)

Manhattan GMAT Prep
the new standard
77

1. The primary purpose of the passage is to

(A) challenge the observation that the Japanese sword is highly admired by historians
(B) introduce new information about the forging of Japanese swords
(C) identify how the Japanese sword is now perceived as much for its artistic qualities as its military ones
(D) argue that Japanese sword makers were as much artists as they were smiths
(E) explain the value attributed to the Japanese sword

To identify the primary purpose of the passage, you should examine the passage as a whole. Avoid answer choices that address only limited sections of the passage.

(A) The passage does not call into question the admiration that historians have for the Japanese sword.

(B) The second paragraph of the passage discusses forging techniques, but none of the information is presented as new. Moreover, these forging techniques are not the focus of the passage.

(C) The artistic merit of the Japanese sword is identified in the last sentence of the second paragraph, but this is not the primary focus of the passage. Much of the passage discusses the sword's physical properties, not the perception of its artistic qualities.

(D) The passage describes some of the similarities between a master smith and an artist; however, these similarities are presented in the second paragraph, and not throughout the passage. Much of the passage describes the Japanese sword's physical properties and reasons for its importance.

(E) CORRECT. The passage as a whole describes the immense value of the Japanese sword to both the samurai (the sword's owner) and the smith (its maker). The saying "The sword is the soul of the samurai" is referenced in the first paragraph to indicate this importance. The second paragraph proceeds to detail the tremendous effort that is put into each sword, reflecting the importance of each one.

2. Each of the following is mentioned in the passage EXCEPT

(A) Every Japanese sword has a unique structure that can be traced back to a special forging process.
(B) Master smiths kept their forging techniques secret.
(C) The Japanese sword was considered by some to have a spiritual quality.
(D) Master smiths are now considered artists by most major historians.
(E) The Japanese sword is now considered as much a work of art as it is a weapon.

the new standard

For an "except" question, you should use the process of elimination to identify and cross out those details mentioned in the passage.

(A) In the passage this "unique signature" is referred to as a "structural signature."

(B) The second paragraph contains the following phrases: "every master smith…due to his own secret forging process."

(C) The first paragraph indicates that "the Japanese sword has always been considered a splendid weapon and even a spiritual entity."

(D) CORRECT. The time and effort master smiths devote to making a sword is discussed, and the passage does indicate that the Japanese sword is considered a unique work of art and of artistic merit. However, the passage does not state that most major historians consider master smiths themselves to be artists. Major historians are not referenced in the passage. Also, the passage states in the second paragraph that "Master smiths may not have been considered artists in the classical sense."

(E) In the last sentence the passage indicates that the Japanese sword is recognized as much for its artistic merit as its historical significance.

    3. The author is most likely to agree with which of the following observations?

    (A) The Japanese sword is the most important handheld weapon in history.
    (B) The skill of the samurai is what made the Japanese sword so special.
    (C) If a sword had a physical signature, other swords could be attributed to that sword's creator.
    (D) Master smiths were more concerned about the artistic merit of their blades than about the blades' practical qualities.
    (E) The Japanese sword has more historical importance than artistic importance.

When looking for statements with which the author could agree, be sure to avoid extreme words and positions that go beyond the author's statements in the passage.

(A) The opening sentence says that "historians have long recognized the Japanese sword as one of the finest cutting weapons ever created"; however, there is no indication that the Japanese sword is the most important handheld weapon in history. There could be many others (e.g. handguns).

(B) This passage does not discuss the skill of the samurai warrior.

(C) CORRECT. In the second paragraph it says every master smith had a "structural signature" due to his own secret forging process. Therefore, if a physical signature is present on a blade, that blade's structural signature could then be associated with a master smith, whose "master" status implies the creation of numerous swords.

(D) The passage mentions that "the sword itself was a reflection of his [the creator's] personal honor and ability"; however, there is no claim that master smiths emphasized their swords' artistic merit at the expense of practical qualities.

(E) The passage acknowledges that the Japanese sword is important both historically and artistically, but the author does not stress the sword's historical importance over its artistry.

4. Which of the following can be inferred about the term "structural signature" in this passage?

(A) It indicates the inscription that the smith places on the blade during the forging process.
(B) It implies the particular characteristics of a blade created by a smith's unique forging process.
(C) It suggests that each blade can be traced back to a known master smith.
(D) It demonstrates the effort and attention that each master smith devoted to the creation of swords.
(E) It refers to the actual curved shape of the blade.

In the second paragraph, the author states that "every master smith had a 'structural signature' due to his own secret forging process." The word "signature" implies the uniqueness of the smith's process. Be careful not to infer any additional information.

(A) In the passage, such an inscription is referred to as a "physical signature," not a "structural signature."

(B) CORRECT. Note that the proof sentence indicates that each smith had his own process, and so the "structural signature" was unique to each smith (not necessarily to each individual blade).

(C) This statement seems reasonable. However, the passage does not say whether all master smiths are currently "known." It is possible that certain swords with a structural signature may be of unknown origin.

(D) The second paragraph mentions the effort and attention to detail involved in the creation of a Japanese sword, but there is no link made to the "structural signature."

(E) The passage does not discuss the shape of the Japanese blade.

5. One function of the second paragraph of the passage is to

(A) present an explanation for a change in perception
(B) determine the historical significance of Japanese swords
(C) explain why each Japanese sword is unique

(D) compare Japanese master smiths to classical artists

(E) review the complete process of making a Japanese sword

To determine the function(s) of any paragraph, pay attention to the emphasized content of the paragraph, in particular any reiterated points, and to the relationship the paragraph has to other paragraphs. In this case, the second paragraph extends the idea introduced in the first paragraph that the Japanese sword is "special" and a "unique work of art."

(A) The second paragraph mentions that Japanese swords are now appreciated more for their artistic merit, but no explanation is provided.

(B) The term "historical significance" closes the second paragraph, but no information is given in the second paragraph to explain or outline that significance.

(C) CORRECT. In several places, the second paragraph underscores the uniqueness of individual Japanese swords. The first sentence mentions that "no sword was created in exactly the same way." Later in the second paragraph, it is mentioned that "every master smith had a 'structural signature'"; finally, the last sentence indicates that "this effort made each blade as unique as the samurai who wielded it."

(D) The passage explains that master smiths were not considered artists in the classical sense, and then goes on to point out the painstaking creation of each sword. This implicitly draws a parallel between the creation of the sword and classical artistry. However, the passage does not actually describe or discuss classical artists, nor does it set forth criteria for classical artists. There is no actual comparison to classical artists, despite the mention of "artistic merit." This answer choice goes too far beyond the passage, and is incorrect.

(E) Elements of the forging process are discussed, but the whole or "complete" process of making a Japanese sword, such as making the handle, polishing the blade, etc. is not discussed in the paragraph.

Answers to Passage B: Television's Invention

In the early years of television, Vladimir Zworykin was, at least in the public sphere, recognized as its inventor. His loudest champion was his boss, David Sarnoff, then president of RCA and a man that we regard even today as "the father of television." Current historians agree that Philo Farnsworth, a self-educated prodigy who was the first to transmit live images, was television's true inventor.

In his own time, Farnsworth's contributions went largely unnoticed, in large part because he was excluded from the process of introducing the invention to a national audience. Sarnoff put televisions into living rooms, and Sarnoff was responsible for a dominant paradigm of the television industry that continues to be relevant today: advertisers pay for the programming so that they can have a receptive audience for their products. Sarnoff had already utilized this construct to develop the radio industry, and it had, within ten years, become ubiquitous. Farnsworth thought the television should be used as an educational tool, but he had little understanding of the business world, and was never able to implement his ideas.

Perhaps one can argue that Sarnoff simply adapted the business model for radio and television from the newspaper industry, replacing the revenue from subscriptions and purchases of individual newspapers with that of selling the television sets themselves, but Sarnoff promoted himself as nothing less than a visionary. Some television critics argue that the construct Sarnoff implemented has played a negative role in determining the content of the programs themselves, while others contend that it merely created a democratic platform from which the audience can determine the types of programming it wants.

This is a SHORT passage (35 lines or fewer on page). Here is a model Headline List:

> Early TV years, Zwork seen as TV inventor but historians agree that
> Farns was true inventor
> --Zwork championed by RCA pres Sarn
>
> Farns excluded from process of introducing TV to public
> --Sarn used advertisers to bring TV to public
> --Farns thought TV should be educational
>
> Perhaps Sarn adapted newspaper model for radio and TV
> --negative for content vs. democratic platform

*Manhattan*GMAT*Prep
the new standard

1. The primary purpose of the passage is to

(A) correct public misconception about Farnsworth's role in developing early television programs
(B) debate the influence of television on popular culture
(C) challenge the current public perception of Vladimir Zworykin
(D) chronicle the events that led up to the invention of the television
(E) describe Sarnoff's influence on the public perception of television's inception, and debate the impact of Sarnoff's paradigm

The answer to a primary purpose question should incorporate elements of the entire passage. Avoid answer choices that address limited sections of the passage.

(A) Farnsworth's influence on the development of the television itself is only mentioned in paragraphs one and two, but not in the last paragraph. Farnsworth's role in developing programs is never mentioned, nor is the correction of a public misconception the focus of the passage.

(B) The impact of television is not discussed until the final paragraph. Although the last paragraph debates whether or not Sarnoff's influence was a positive one, it does not address the influence of television on popular culture.

(C) Vladimir Zworykin is only mentioned briefly in the first paragraph, so he is clearly not the primary subject of the passage. Furthermore, even though we know the initial public perception, we know nothing about the current public perception of Zworykin.

(D) The passage discusses events that occurred after the invention; there is no mention of the events that led up to the invention of the television.

(E) CORRECT. This answer includes the main elements of all three paragraphs, and is a good summary of the entire passage.

2. It can be inferred from the third paragraph of the passage that

(A) television shows produced by David Sarnoff and Vladimir Zworykin tended to earn negative reviews
(B) educational programs cannot draw as large an audience as sports programs
(C) a number of critics feel that Sarnoff's initial decision to earn television revenue through advertising has had a positive or neutral impact on content
(D) educational programs that are aired in prime time, the hours during which the greatest number of viewers are watching television, are less likely to earn a profit than those that are aired during the daytime hours
(E) in matters of programming, the audience's preferences should be more influential than those of the advertisers

All of the choices reflect an interpretation of the third paragraph. That paragraph states that some critics viewed Sarnoff's paradigm negatively and others thought it embodied a democratic concept. The correct answer must follow from those statements.

(A) We have been given no information about the television programs Sarnoff and Zworykin produced; in fact, we haven't been told that they produced television shows. The paragraph is about the advertising revenue construct Sarnoff implemented, not about the television shows he produced.

(B) It is implied that ratings for educational programs are, in general, not strong, but that does not mean that any one particular educational program can't have higher ratings than one particular sports program. Beware of answer choices that contain absolutes such as "cannot."

(C) CORRECT. We are told that "some television critics argue that Sarnoff's paradigm has played a negative role in determining the content." Since it is only some, it must be true that others either feel it has played a positive role, or a neutral role.

(D) The passage does not differentiate programming based on what time television shows air, nor does it mention profitability.

(E) The word "should" implies a moral judgment, and the answer is therefore out of the scope of the passage. Furthermore, the third paragraph does not indicate a belief as to who should properly influence programming choices.

3. **Which of the following best illustrates the relationship between the second and third paragraphs?**

   (A) The second paragraph dissects the evolution of a contemporary controversy; the third paragraph presents differing viewpoints on that controversy.
   (B) The second paragraph explores the antithetical intentions of two men involved in the infancy of an industry; the third paragraph details the eventual deterioration of that industry.
   (C) The second paragraph presents differing views of a historical event; the third paragraph represents the author's personal opinion about that event.
   (D) The second paragraph provides details that are necessary to support the author's opinion, which is presented in the third paragraph.
   (E) The second paragraph presents divergent visions about the possible uses of a technological device; the third paragraph initiates a debate about the ramifications of one of those perspectives.

The second paragraph presents the differences between Sarnoff and Farnsworth's perspectives. The third paragraph presents differing points of view on the impact that Sarnoff's paradigm has had. The correct answer will incorporate those points.

(A) It is unclear what "contemporary controversy" the second paragraph explores. The second paragraph is about the differences between Sarnoff and Farnsworth--these differences do

not represent a controversy nor are they contemporary. The third paragraph presents differing points of view about the impact that Sarnoff's paradigm has had. The differing points of view are not related to the material in the second paragraph.

(B) Though they had different visions of what television could be, Farnsworth and Sarnoff did not have visions that were "antithetical," or the opposites of each other. Additionally, there is no evidence presented in the third paragraph that alludes to the deterioration of the television industry.

(C) In the second paragraph, we are given differing visions of what could be, not differing opinions of something that has already happened. The author provides opposing viewpoints, but refrains from presenting his own.

(D) The author provides opposing viewpoints, but refrains from presenting his own opinion in the passage.

(E) CORRECT. The second paragraph expresses two different visions of how to use the television; the third paragraph explores the impact of the adoption of Sarnoff's vision.

> **4. According to the passage, the television industry, at its inception, earned revenue from**
>
>   (A) advertising only
>   (B) advertising and the sale of television sets
>   (C) advertising and subscriptions
>   (D) subscriptions and the sale of television sets
>   (E) advertising, subscriptions, and the sale of television sets

Two sections in the passage discuss ways in which the television industry brought in revenue. The second paragraph states that "advertisers pay for the programming so that they can have a receptive audience for their products." The third paragraph states that the television industry benefited by "replacing the revenue from subscriptions and purchases of individual newspapers with that of selling the television sets themselves."

(A) This answer choice does not account for the revenue generated from selling television sets.

(B) CORRECT. Advertising and the sale of television sets are the two ways mentioned through which the industry could generate revenue.

(C) Subscriptions are mentioned as a method for newspapers to earn revenue; the last paragraph clearly states that television replaced this revenue with that earned by selling the sets themselves.

(D) This choice does not mention advertising revenue, and incorrectly mentions subscription revenue.

(E) This answer choice incorrectly mentions subscription revenue.

5. **The passage suggests that Farnsworth might have earned greater public notoriety for his invention if**

    (A) Vladimir Zworykin had been less vocal about his own contributions to the television

    (B) Farnsworth had been able to develop and air his own educational programs

    (C) Farnsworth had involved Sarnoff in his plans to develop, manufacture, or distribute the television

    (D) Sarnoff had involved Farnsworth in his plans to develop, manufacture, or distribute the television

    (E) Farnsworth had a better understanding of the type of programming the audience wanted to watch most

Farnsworth's notoriety, or lack thereof, is discussed at the beginning of the second paragraph, where it is written, "In his own time, Farnsworth's contributions went largely unnoticed, in large part because he was excluded from the process of introducing the invention to a national audience." Thus, the passage clearly suggests that if he had been included in that process of introducing the invention, his contributions would have been noticed more widely.

(A) There is no mention made of Zworykin being vocal about his own contributions. Furthermore, the passage hints at no connection between Zworykin's self-promotion and Farnsworth's lack of notoriety.

(B) Though we have been told that Farnsworth wanted to use television as an educational tool, we have not been told that he wanted to develop television shows himself. Additionally, it is debatable whether the development of educational television programs would have significantly contributed to Farnsworth's public notoriety.

(C) The passage states that Farnsworth was the one who was excluded, not the one who prevented others from getting involved.

(D) CORRECT. The passage states that Farnsworth's contributions went unnoticed partly because he was excluded from the process of introducing the invention to the audience. If he had been involved in the development, manufacture, or distribution, he would have been involved in the introduction process, and it logically follows that this could have led to greater notoriety.

(E) The passage does not connect Farnsworth's lack of notoriety with a lack of understanding about the television audience, nor does it state in any way Farnsworth's opinions about the audience.

Answers to Passage C: Life on Mars

Because of the proximity and likeness of Mars to Earth, scientists have long speculated about the possibility of life on Mars. As early as the mid-17th century, astronomers observed polar ice caps on Mars, and by the mid-19th century, scientists discovered other similarities to Earth, including the length of day and axial tilt. But in 1965, photos taken by the Mariner 4 probe revealed a Mars without rivers, oceans or signs of life. And in the 1990s, it was discovered that Mars, unlike Earth, no longer possessed a substantial global magnetic field, allowing celestial radiation to reach the planet's surface and solar wind to eliminate much of Mars's atmosphere over the course of several billion years.

More recent probes have focused on whether there was once water on Mars. Some scientists believe that this question is definitively answered by the presence of certain geological landforms. Others posit that different explanations, such as wind erosion or carbon dioxide oceans, may be responsible for these formations. Mars rovers Opportunity and Spirit, which have been exploring the surface of Mars since 2004, have both discovered geological evidence of past water activity. These findings substantially bolster claims that there was once life on Mars.

This is a SHORT passage (35 lines or fewer on page). Here is a model Headline List:

S: proximity and similarity of Mars to Earth → possible life on Mars
--similarities (polar ice caps, day, tilt)
--differences (no water, no longer subst magnetic field)

More recent focus on whether there once was water on mars; evidence suggests there was
(geological landforms)

1. The author's stance on the possibility of life on Mars can best be described as

(A) optimistic
(B) disinterested
(C) skeptical
(D) simplistic
(E) cynical

This passage is concerned with the possibility of life on Mars. It details the various discoveries that have been made since the mid-17th century. The passage can best be described as factual and unbiased. In considering the answer choices, you should remember to avoid extreme words.

(A) The author is neither optimistic nor pessimistic about the possibility of life on Mars.

(B) CORRECT. Note that disinterested, meaning neutral, is different from uninterested, meaning bored and indifferent.

(C) There is no indication that the author of the passage is skeptical. The passage simply puts forth facts and does not offer an opinion one way or the other.

(D) The author considers several different factors in the determination of life on Mars. The author's stance could not appropriately be described as simplistic.

(E) Again, the author is objective in tone, and could not accurately be characterized as cynical.

2. The passage is primarily concerned with which of the following?

(A) disproving a widely accepted theory
(B) initiating a debate about the possibility of life on Mars
(C) presenting evidence in support of a controversial claim
(D) describing the various discoveries made concerning the possibility of life on
　　　Mars
(E) detailing the findings of the Mars rovers Opportunity and Spirit

This passage is primarily concerned with the possibility of life on Mars. The two paragraphs discuss various discoveries that have been made over the past several centuries. The passage concludes that recent findings substantiate claims that there was once life on Mars. However, scientists are still not certain. In determining the purpose or main idea of the passage, it is important to avoid extreme words and to be able to defend every word.

(A) This passage does not set out to disprove the theory that there is life on Mars. It is also too extreme to suggest that this is a widely accepted theory.

(B) This answer choice is tempting because it is relatively neutral. However, the passage does

*Manhattan*GMAT Prep
the new standard

not seek to initiate a debate; it is more concerned with documenting findings pertaining to life on Mars. In other words, the passage is presenting the findings that frame a debate, not initiating the debate itself.

(C) The passage presents evidence in support of and against the possibility of life on Mars. It is too limited to suggest that the passage is primarily concerned with presenting evidence in support of life of Mars.

(D) CORRECT. This answer choice avoids extreme words and best summarizes the purpose of the passage.

(E) This answer choice is too specific. The passage does mention the Mars rovers Opportunity and Spirit, but it is inaccurate to suggest that the passage is primarily concerned with these two rovers.

3. Each of the following discoveries is mentioned in the passage EXCEPT

> (A) Wind erosion and carbon dioxide oceans are responsible for certain geological landforms on Mars.
> (B) Mars does not have a substantial global magnetic field.
> (C) Mars does not currently have water activity.
> (D) The length of day on Mars is similar to that on Earth.
> (E) The axial tilt of Mars is similar to that of Earth.

This is a specific question; it is helpful to point to specific evidence in the text to defend your answer choice. The passage discusses several discoveries; to answer this question, find which of the answer choices is NOT a discovery specifically mentioned in the passage.

(A) CORRECT. The passage does make mention of wind erosion and carbon dioxide oceans, but the author states that these are other possible explanations for certain geological landforms on Mars. Wind erosion and carbon dioxide oceans are possible causes of the geological landforms rather than discoveries.

(B) At the end of the first paragraph, the passage states, "in the 1990s, it was discovered that Mars, unlike Earth, no longer possessed a substantial global magnetic field."

(C) The Mariner 4 probe revealed in 1965 that there are no rivers or oceans (water activity) on Mars in the third sentence of the first paragraph.

(D) Certain similarities of Mars to Earth were discovered in the mid-19th century, including the length of day in the second sentence of the first paragraph.

(E) Certain similarities of Mars to Earth were discovered in the mid-19th century, including the axial tilt of Mars being similar to that of the Earth in the second sentence of the first paragraph.

4. In the first paragraph, the author most likely mentions the discovery of polar ice caps to suggest that

(A) until recently Mars' polar ice caps were thought to consist largely of carbon dioxide
(B) Martian polar ice caps are made almost entirely of water ice
(C) Mars has many similarities to Earth, including the existence of polar ice caps
(D) Mars has only a small fraction of the carbon dioxide found on Earth and Venus
(E) conditions on the planet Mars were once very different than they are at present

This is a specific question that refers back to the second sentence in the first paragraph. The best approach is to reread this sentence and determine, using surrounding sentences if necessary, what the author's purpose is in mentioning Mars' polar ice caps. If we read the second part of the sentence, "by the mid-19th century, scientists discovered other similarities to Earth, including the length of day and axial tilt," we notice that polar ice caps are introduced as an example of the similarity of Mars to Earth.

(A) The passage does not mention the content of the polar ice caps, just that they were observed.

(B) Again, we do not know, from the passage, the composition of Mars' polar ice caps.

(C) CORRECT. As stated above, polar ice caps are introduced as one of several similarities of Mars to Earth.

(D) The passage does not indicate the carbon dioxide content or Mars or Earth. It also does not mention Venus.

(E) While we know from the rest of the passage that conditions on Mars were probably different than they are now, the author does not mention polar ice caps in order to indicate this.

5. Each of the following can be inferred from the passage EXCEPT

(A) The presence of certain geological landforms is not definitive proof that there was once life on Mars.
(B) It is likely that there were few significant discoveries related to the possibility of life on Mars prior to the mid-17th century.
(C) The absence of a substantial global magnetic field on Mars suggests that it would be difficult to sustain life on Mars.
(D) The presence of water activity on Mars is related to the possibility of life on Mars.
(E) The claim that there was once water on Mars has only limited and indirect support from recent discoveries.

A question that asks for an inference from the passage is a specific question; it is helpful to find evidence for any inference in the text. Make sure each inference can be defended by going back to the text, and does not go far beyond the language in the passage.

(A) In the second paragraph, the author states that while the presence of geological landforms may indicate the presence of water, it is also possible that these landforms were caused by wind erosion or carbon dioxide oceans.

(B) The first discoveries mentioned were as early as the mid-17th century. Therefore, it is reasonable to conclude that it is likely that there were not many significant discoveries before this time. Notice that this inference avoids extreme words: It does not say that there were no discoveries, just that it is not "likely" that many preceded this period.

(C) In the second paragraph, the absence of a substantial global magnetic field is presented as evidence of the lack of life on Mars. Again, note that this answer choice avoids extreme words by using the word "suggests."

(D) The first sentence in the second paragraph states that "more recent probes have focused on whether or not there was once water on Mars." Given this purpose, it is clear that the existence of water is important in order to establish whether or not there was life on Mars.

(E) CORRECT. According to the second paragraph, the Mars rovers Opportunity and Spirit "have both discovered geological evidence of past water activity." This is both significant (as made clear by the subsequent sentence that "these findings substantially bolster claims... ") and direct evidence supporting the claim that there was once water on Mars. Thus, the passage contradicts the statement that this claim is supported by only limited and indirect evidence.

Answers to Passage D: Fossils

In archaeology, as with the physical sciences, new discoveries frequently undermine accepted findings and give rise to new theories. This can be seen in the reaction to the recent discovery of a set of 3.3-million-year-old fossils in Ethiopia that comprise the earliest well-preserved child ever found. The fossilized child was estimated to be about 3 years old at death, female, and a member of the Australopithecus afarensis species. The afarensis species, a major human ancestor, lived in Africa from earlier than 3.7 million to 3 million years ago. "Her completeness, antiquity and age at death make this find of unprecedented importance in the history of paleo-anthropology," said Zeresenay Alemseged, a noted paleo-anthropologist. Other scientists said that the discovery could reconfigure conceptions about the lives and capacities of these early humans.

Prior to this discovery, it had been thought that the afarensis species had abandoned the arboreal habitat of their ape cousins. However, while the lower limbs of this fossil supported findings that afarensis walked upright, its gorilla-like arms and shoulders suggested that it retained the ability to swing through trees. This has initiated a reexamination of many accepted theories of early human development. Also, the presence of a hyoid bone, a rarely preserved bone in the larynx that supports muscles of the throat, has had a tremendous impact on theories about the origins of speech. The fossil bone is primitive and more similar to those of apes than humans, but it is the first hyoid found in such an early human-related species.

This is a SHORT passage (35 lines or fewer on page). Here is a model Headline List:

In archeology, new discoveries → undermine findings, lead to new theories
--(child fossils of Afar. species in Ethiopia)

Prior to discovery: Afar. had abandoned arboreal habitat of apes
Presence of hyoid bone impacted theories of speech

1. The organization of the passage could best be described as

(A) discussing a controversial scientific discovery
(B) contrasting previous theories of development with current findings
(C) illustrating a contention with a specific example
(D) arguing the importance of a particular field of study
(E) refuting a popular misconception

This passage begins by noting that new discoveries frequently undermine accepted findings and give rise to new theories in archaeology. It supports this statement by relating the impact of one discovery in the field. Thus, the best answer will reference both the contention and the use of the example.

(A) This choice omits the phenomenon that the discovery is meant to illustrate, which is that discoveries often give rise to new theories. Also, there is nothing controversial about the described discovery.

(B) The passage does not focus on the contrast between previous theories of development and current findings. Rather, it discusses a singular discovery that affects previous theories. This answer choice omits mention of the example of the specific discovery, which is a fundamental part of the structure.

(C) CORRECT. The passage makes a claim and uses a specific example to support that claim, just as this choice states.

(D) The passage does not argue for the importance of archaeology as a field of study. This answer choice misstates the organization of the passage.

(E) The earlier theories of human development are too esoteric to be properly classified as a "popular misconception." Also, the passage is organized around the example of a single discovery and its importance, not the refutation of past theories.

2. The passage quotes Zeresenay Alemseged in order to

(A) provide evidence to support the main idea of the first paragraph
(B) question the claims of other scientists
(C) provide evidence to support the linguistic abilities of the afarensis species
(D) provide evidence that supports the significance of the find
(E) provide a subjective opinion that is refuted in the second paragraph

This quotation in the first paragraph highlights the importance of the discovery and is followed by another similar reference. The quotation is used to emphasize the exceptional importance of this find; the correct answer will reflect this emphasis.

(A) The main idea of the first paragraph is that a new finding can call accepted archaeological theories into question, and to provide an example of this phenomenon. The quotation emphasizes the importance of the discussed discovery; this is not the main idea of the first paragraph.

(B) The passage does not discuss claims of other scientists that the discovered fossils are not important. Therefore, this answer choice is incorrect.

(C) The discussion of the linguistic ability of the afarensis species is in the second paragraph and is unrelated to this quotation.

(D) CORRECT. The point of this paragraph is to illustrate that archeology is more like a physical science in that important factual discoveries lead to theoretical changes. The quotation provides evidence that this discovery is in fact a significant one.

(E) The quotation is offered as evidence of the importance of the discovery, and is not refuted at any point in the passage.

3. **Each of the following is cited as a factor in the importance of the discovery of the fossils EXCEPT**

(A) the fact that the remains were those of a child
(B) the age of the fossils
(C) the location of the discovery
(D) the species of the fossils
(E) the intact nature of the fossils

With a question of this sort, instead of looking for the correct answer, it is often easier to eliminate incorrect answer choices based on the information provided in the passage.

(A) The fifth sentence of the first paragraph cites a quotation from a noted paleo-anthropologist that the find of the child fossils was of unprecedented importance due to the child's "age at death." Therefore, the fact that the remains were those of a child was of substantial significance.

(B) The "antiquity" of the fossils is mentioned in the first paragraph as a reason why the fossils were an important discovery.

(C) CORRECT. The location of the fossil discovery is mentioned in the first paragraph of the passage. However, the location is not provided as a reason why the fossils are significant.

(D) The fossils are described in the second paragraph of the passage as impacting "accepted theories of early human development." The fossils are also shown to be important to the development of speech. These implications would not be applicable if the fossils were not of a species of human ancestor (e.g. the fossils of an ancient elephant). Also, there were specific preconceptions of the afarensis species that were called into question by the discovery of the fossils. Thus, the species of the fossils is of particular significance to the discovery.

(E) The fifth sentence of the first paragraph notes that the find was important due its "completeness." The intact nature of the fossils is another way of saying that the fossils are complete.

4. It can be inferred from the passage's description of the discovered fossil hyoid bone that

(A) Australopithecus afarensis were capable of speech
(B) the discovered hyoid bone is less primitive than the hyoid bone of apes
(C) the hyoid bone is necessary for speech
(D) the discovery of the hyoid bone necessitated the reexamination of prior theories
(E) the hyoid bone was the most important fossil found at the site

The passage provides the following information about the discovered hyoid bone: it is the oldest ever found since the bone is rarely preserved and it "is primitive and more similar to those of apes than humans." The passage also states the discovery will impact theories about speech. A good inference is a point that must follow from one of these statements.

(A) The passage gives no information about the linguistic capacities of Australopithecus afarensis. The passage does not give enough information to infer that they were capable of speech.

(B) The passage indicates that the discovered hyoid bone more closely resembles those of apes than humans, but it is not the case that the discovered bone is necessarily less primitive than that of an ape. It could be slightly different in a way that is equally primitive; not all differences in structure would make a bone more advanced.

(C) While it can be inferred that this bone has an effect on speech, the passage does not indicate that it is necessary for speech. It is possible that a modern species could be capable of speech without a hyoid bone.

(D) CORRECT. The passage states that the discovery of the hyoid bone "has had a tremendous impact on theories about the origins of speech." The passage goes on to say that it is the first hyoid found in such an early human-related species, suggesting that the timeline of human verbal development would be changed by the discovery. Thus, it can be inferred that the discovery made the reexamination of prior theories necessary.

(E) The passage does not rank the importance of the fossils found; as a result, this choice is not necessarily correct. It is possible that other fossils were of equal or greater importance.

5. According to the passage, the impact of the discovery of the hyoid bone in the field of archaeology could best be compared to which one of the following examples in another field?

(A) The discovery and analysis of cosmic rays lend support to a widely accepted theory of the origin of the universe.

*Manhattan*GMAT Prep

(B) The original manuscript of a deceased 19th century author confirms ideas of the development of an important work of literature.

(C) The continued prosperity of a state-run economy stirs debate in the discipline of macroeconomics.

(D) Newly revealed journal entries by a prominent Civil War era politician lead to a questioning of certain accepted historical interpretations about the conflict.

(E) Research into the mapping of the human genome gives rise to nascent applications of individually tailored medicines.

The passage indicates that the discovery of the hyoid bone "has initiated a reexamination of many accepted theories of early human development." Additionally, the discovery is described as having "had a tremendous impact on theories about the origins of speech." These sentences indicate that the discovery of the hyoid bone has either expanded or called into question certain previously held ideas in the field. The correct answer will reflect this sort of impact in another field.

(A) This answer choice discusses the impact of the discovery and analysis of cosmic rays on the field of physics. However, in this example the discovery serves to support a widely accepted theory, as opposed to causing a reexamination of earlier ideas.

(B) This answer choice describes the original manuscript of an author that confirms ideas of the development of an important work of literature. However, in this answer choice the discovery serves to confirm earlier held ideas, as opposed to causing a reexamination of accepted ideas.

(C) This answer choice describes a current phenomenon, the continued success of a state-run economy, that stirs debate in the discipline of macroeconomics. This example is dissimilar from the discovery of the hyoid bone in a number of ways. First, the success of a state-run economy is a contemporary phenomenon rather than a discovery. Also, the provocation of debate is not analogous to a "reexamination of accepted theories," as there is no indication that an accepted macroeconomic theory is applicable and being called into question. Last, the state-run economy in question could be the latest example in a long line of successful controlled economies, as opposed to being a discovery of any importance.

(D) CORRECT. This answer choice correctly describes a discovery that causes a reexamination of earlier ideas in another field. In this case, newly uncovered journal entries by a politician spur a re-evaluation of certain historical ideas regarding an important conflict.

(E) This answer choice describes scientific advances in the field of biology as giving rise to new applications. It does not discuss a discovery that calls accepted ideas into question.

Answers to Passage E: Polygamy

Polygamy in Africa has been a popular topic for social research over the past four decades; it has been analyzed by many distinguished minds and in various well-publicized works. In 1961, when Remi Clignet published his book "Many Wives, Many Powers," he was not alone in sharing the view that in Africa co-wives may be perceived as direct and indirect sources of increased income and prestige.

By the 1970s, such arguments had become crystallized and popular. Many other African scholars who wrote on the subject became the new champions of this philosophy. For example, in 1983, John Mbiti proclaimed that polygamy is an accepted and respectable institution serving many useful social purposes. Similarly, G.K. Nukunya, in his paper "Polygamy as a Symbol of Status," reiterated Mbiti's idea that a plurality of wives is a sign of affluence and power in the African society.

However, the colonial missionary voice provided one consistent opposition to polygamy by viewing the practice as unethical and destructive of family life. While they propagated this view with the authority of the Bible, they were convinced that Africans had to be coerced into partaking in the vision of monogamy understood by the Western culture. The missionary viewpoint even included, in some instances, dictating immediate divorce in the case of newly converted men who had already contracted polygamous marriages. Unfortunately, both the missionary voice and the scholarly voice did not consider the views of African women on the matter important. Although there was some awareness that women regarded polygamy as both a curse and a blessing, the distanced, albeit scientific, perspective of an outside observer predominated both on the pulpit and in scholarly writings.

Contemporary research in the social sciences has begun to focus on the protagonist's voice in the study of culture, recognizing that the views and experiences of those who take part in a given reality ought to receive close examination. This privileging of the protagonist seems appropriate, particularly given that women in Africa have often used literary productions to comment on marriage, family and gender relations.

This is a LONG passage (more than 35 lines on page). Here is a model Skeletal Sketch:

<u>Past 4 decades: Polygamy in Africa popular topic for social research</u>
1961: Clignet book views co-wives as source of income and prestige

Scholarly view of polygamy as serving useful social purpose and signal of wealth and power is crystallized in 1970s and 1980s

Missionary voice opposed polygamy but neither it nor scholars considered view of African women important

Contemporary research focuses on experiences of protagonists such as African women

---

1. **Which of the following best describes the main purpose of the passage above?**

   (A) to discuss scholarly works that view polygamy as a sign of prestige, respect, and affluence in the African society
   (B) to trace the origins of the missionary opposition to African polygamy
   (C) to argue for imposing restrictions on polygamy in the African society
   (D) to explore the reasons for women's acceptance of polygamy
   (E) to discuss multiple perspectives on African polygamy and contrast them with contemporary research

On questions asking about the main idea of the passage, be sure to avoid extreme answer choices and those answers that refer to a part of the passage rather than the whole text. Typically, test writers will include several incorrect answers that will be factually true but will describe the purpose of just one paragraph rather than the text as a whole.

(A) Scholarly works that view polygamy as a sign of prestige and affluence are discussed only in the first two paragraphs of the passage. This answer is too narrow to capture the purpose of the entire text.

(B) While the third paragraph discusses the missionary opposition and traces its sources to the Bible, this analysis is not central to the entire passage and is thus too narrow to capture the scope of the entire text.

(C) While the text discusses multiple perspectives on polygamy, it does not argue in favor or against restricting polygamy.

(D) The passage provides no information about the reasons that women accept polygamy, other than mentioning that they view it as both "a curse and a blessing."

(E) CORRECT. The entire passage is devoted to the discussion of multiple perspectives on polygamy. The first two paragraphs review scholarly works that view polygamy as a sign of prestige and respect; the third paragraph offers an opposing view; finally, the concluding paragraph contrasts both of these perspectives with contemporary research.

2. **The third paragraph of the passage plays which of the following roles?**

(A) discusses the rationale for viewing polygamy as an indication of prestige and affluence in the African society
(B) supports the author's view that polygamy is unethical and destructive of family life
(C) contrasts the views of the colonial missionary with the position of the most recent contemporary research
(D) describes the views on polygamy held by the colonial missionary and indicates a flaw in this vision
(E) demonstrates that the colonial missionary was ignorant of the scholarly research on monogamy

This question asks us to summarize the role of the third paragraph. On this type of question, it is helpful to re-read the topic sentence of the paragraph at issue. The topic sentence is typically in the first or second sentence of the paragraph. Furthermore, look for the answer that effectively captures the entire paragraph and avoids making unjustified statements.

(A) These scholarly works are discussed in the first and second rather than the third paragraph.

(B) While the third paragraph discusses the views of the colonial missionary, nothing in the passage suggests that the author shares this vision.

(C) While the third paragraph presents the position of the colonial missionary, the most recent contemporary research is discussed only in the concluding paragraph of the passage.

(D) CORRECT. The second paragraph describes the position of the colonial missionary and indicates a flaw in this perspective. Note that this idea is mimicked in the opening sentence of the paragraph: "However, the colonial missionary voice provided one consistent opposition to polygamy by viewing the practice as unethical and destructive of family life." Furthermore, after discussing this position, the author goes on to identify a deficiency in this reasoning: "Unfortunately, both the missionary voice and the scholarly voice did not consider the views of African women on the matter important."

(E) While the third paragraph discusses the perspective of the colonial missionary, nothing is mentioned in the passage about the attitude of the missionary towards scholarly research on monogamy.

3. The passage provides each of the following, EXCEPT

(A) the year of publication of Remi Clignet's book "Many Wives, Many Powers"
(B) the year in which John Mbiti made a claim that polygamy is an accepted institution
(C) examples of African women's literary productions devoted to family relations
(D) reasons for missionary opposition to polygamy
(E) current research perspectives on polygamy

On detail questions, you can facilitate your decision process by looking for signal words. Since this is an "except" question, we can answer it by findings the statements that were mentioned in the passage and eliminating them from our consideration set. In this process, make sure to use proper nouns (such as Remi Clignet) and dates (such as 1983) as your signals. Since dates and capitalized nouns stand out in the text, they can speed up the process of verifying the answer choices.

(A) The second sentence of the opening paragraph states that Remi Clignet published his book "Many Wives, Many Powers" in 1961.

(B) According to the second sentence of the second paragraph, John Mbiti proclaimed that polygamy is an accepted and respectable institution in 1983.

(C) CORRECT. According to the third paragraph, "both the missionary voice and the scholarly voice did not consider the views of African women on the matter as important." The concluding paragraph mentions that "women in Africa have often used literary productions to comment on marriage" but provides no specific examples of such works.

(D) According to the third paragraph of the passage, the colonial missionary opposed polygamy because it considered this practice "as unethical and destructive of family life."

(E) The opening sentence of the last paragraph provides a detailed description of the position of contemporary research towards polygamy.

4. According to the passage, the colonial missionary and the early scholarly research shared which of the following traits in their views on polygamy?

(A) both considered polygamy a sign of social status and success
(B) neither accounted for the views of local women
(C) both attempted to limit the prevalence of polygamy
(D) both pointed out polygamy's destructive effects on family life
(E) both exhibited a somewhat negative attitude towards polygamy

*Manhattan*GMAT*Prep
the new standard

To answer this detail question, we need to refer to paragraph three, which offers a comparison of the views of the colonial missionary and those of early scholars. Note that the correct answer will outline the trait that was shared by both groups, while incorrect answers will typically restate characteristics that were true of only one rather than both groups.

(A) While the early scholarly researchers indeed viewed polygamy as a sign of prestige, this perspective was not shared by the colonial missionary, who declared it "unethical and destructive of family life."

(B) CORRECT. This statement is explicitly supported by the penultimate sentence of the third paragraph: "Unfortunately, both the missionary voice and the scholarly voice did not consider the views of African women on the matter important."

(C) While the passage suggests that the colonial missionary may have attempted to limit the prevalence of polygamy by coercing Africans "into partaking in the vision of monogamy," nothing in the passage suggests that the scholarly research shared this perspective.

(D) This view was characteristic of the colonial missionary, as discussed in the third paragraph, but not of the early scholarly research.

(E) According to the third paragraph, the colonial missionary certainly maintained a negative attitude towards polygamy, considering this practice "unethical and destructive of family life." By contrast, early scholarly research considered this phenomenon "a sign of affluence and power." Nothing in the passage suggests that the early scholars had a negative attitude towards polygamy.

5. **Which of the following statements can most confidently be inferred from the passage?**

(A) Nukunya's paper "Polygamy as a Symbol of Status" was not written in 1981.
(B) John Mbiti adjusted his initial view on polygamy, recognizing that the experiences of African women should receive closer attention.
(C) Remi Clignet's book "Many Wives, Many Powers" was the first well-known scholarly work to proclaim that polygamy can be viewed as a symbol or prestige and wealth.
(D) Under the influence of the missionary opposition, polygamy was proclaimed illegal in Africa as a practice "unethical and destructive of family life."
(E) A large proportion of the scholars writing on polygamy in the 1970s and 1980s were of African descent.

Since this is an inference question, we will be looking for an answer that can be inferred strictly based on the information given in the passage and without making any additional assumptions. Typically, the correct answer must be very closely connected to the actual text of the passage and directly supported by one or two sentences. Also, be sure to avoid inferences that may be seen as plausible but would require information not provided in the passage.

(A) **CORRECT.** The second paragraph states that Nukunya's work "Polygamy as a Symbol of Status" "reiterated Mbiti's idea that that plurality of wives is a sign of affluence and power...". Since Nukunya's work reiterated the views of Mbiti, "Polygamy as a Symbol of Status" must have been written after Mbiti expressed his perspective on polygamy. According to the text, it was not until 1983 that "John Mbiti proclaimed that polygamy is an accepted and respectable institution." Therefore, Nukunya's "Polygamy as a Symbol of Status" must have been written after 1983, and we can conclude that it was not written in 1981.

(B) While the text mentions that contemporary research acknowledges that the perspective of African women should receive closer attention, nothing in the passage suggests that Mbiti subsequently embraced this view and changed his initial stance.

(C) In the second sentence of the opening paragraph, the author states that "when Remi Clignet published his book 'Many Wives, Many Powers,' he was not alone in sharing the view...," suggesting that at the time of publication, there were other scholarly works that viewed polygamy as a symbol or prestige and wealth. Therefore, Clignet's book was not the first to give this perspective.

(D) While the passage mentions that the colonial missionary opposed polygamy, viewing it as "unethical and destructive," nothing in the passage suggests that polygamy was declared illegal in Africa.

(E) The passage provides no information regarding the background of the scholars who wrote about African polygamy. Moreover, even if this information were provided for the several examples of scholarly work mentioned in the passage, it would not be possible to make any conclusions about the scholars not mentioned in the passage.

Answers to Passage F: Sweet Spot

Though most tennis players generally strive to strike the ball on the racket's vibration node, more commonly known as the "sweet spot," many players are unaware of the existence of a second, lesser-known location on the racket face, the center of percussion, that will also greatly diminish the strain on a player's arm when the ball is struck.

In order to understand the physics of this second sweet spot, it is helpful to consider what would happen to a tennis racket in the moments after impact with the ball if the player's hand were to vanish at the moment of impact. The impact of the ball would cause the racket to bounce backwards, experiencing a translational motion away from the ball. The tendency of this motion would be to jerk all parts of the racket, including the end of its handle, backward, or away from the ball. Unless the ball happened to hit the racket precisely at the racket's center of mass, the racket would additionally experience a rotational motion around its center of mass – much as a penny that has been struck near its edge will start to spin. The effect of this rotational motion would be to jerk the end of the handle forward, towards the ball. Depending on where the ball struck the racket face, one or the other of these motions would predominate.

However, there is one point of impact, known as the center of percussion, which causes neither motion to predominate; if a ball were to strike this point, the impact would not impart any motion to the end of the handle. The reason for this lack of motion is that the force on the upper part of the hand would be equal and opposite to the force on the lower part of the hand, resulting in no net force on the tennis players' hand or forearm. The center of percussion constitutes a second sweet spot because a tennis player's wrist typically is placed next to the end of the racket's handle. When the player strikes the ball at the center of percussion, her wrist is jerked neither forward nor backward, and she experiences a relatively smooth, comfortable tennis stroke.

The manner in which a tennis player can detect the center of percussion on a given tennis racket follows from the nature of this second sweet spot. The center of percussion can be located via simple trial and error by holding the end of a tennis racket between your finger and thumb and throwing a ball onto the strings. If the handle jumps out of your hand, then the ball missed the center of percussion.

This is a LONG passage (more than 35 lines on page). Here is a model Skeletal Sketch:

Tennis players try to strike ball on racket's vibration node or sweet spot
<u>Many players unaware of second spot, CP, that also diminishes arm strain</u>

Assuming no hand, when ball hits racket one of two forces--backwards motion or rotational motion that jerks handle forward--predominates

If ball hits CP, neither motion predominates so player's wrist is not jerked forward or backward

CP can be found on racket using trial & error by understanding what CP is

---

1. **What is the primary message the author is trying to convey?**

    (A) a proposal for an improvement to the design of tennis rackets
    (B) an examination of the differences between the two types of sweet spot
    (C) a definition of the translational and rotational forces acting on a tennis racket
    (D) a description of the ideal area in which to strike every ball
    (E) an explanation of a lesser-known area on a tennis racket that dampens unwanted vibration

The first paragraph introduces the idea that there are two sweet spots on the face of a tennis racket: one well-known spot and another lesser-known spot. The sweet spots are defined as the impact areas which will diminish the vibrations or tremors that can transfer from the racket to the player's arm. The second and third paragraphs detail how the mechanism of the second sweet spot, the center of percussion, works. The fourth paragraph describes a way to find the center of percussion.

(A) Nothing in the passage suggests that the author is trying to propose an improvement to the design of tennis rackets. The second sweet spot exists independent of the design of the racket.

(B) The passage does mention both types of sweet spot in the first paragraph, but it does not focus on the differences between the two.

(C) Paragraph two explains the types of forces acting on the racket, but this topic is too narrow to be the primary message of the overall passage. The passage as a whole focuses on the sweet spots as opposed to the forces acting on the racket.

(D) While the passage does mention one benefit of hitting the ball on a sweet spot, it does not claim that this is the "ideal" area to hit "every" ball. There may be other areas that convey other benefits. In addition, "every" is too extreme.

(E) CORRECT. This matches our initial summary, above: the passage introduces the notion of a "second, lesser-known" sweet spot which can also "diminish the strain" when a player strikes the ball.

2. **According to the passage, all of the following are true of the forces acting upon a tennis racket striking a ball EXCEPT**

(A) The only way to eliminate the jolt that accompanies most strokes is to hit the ball on the center of percussion.
(B) The impact of the ball striking the racket can strain a tennis player's arm.
(C) There are at least two different forces acting upon the racket.
(D) The end of the handle of the racket will jerk forward after striking the ball unless the ball strikes the racket's center of mass.
(E) The racket will rebound after it strikes the ball.

"Except" questions require us to validate the answer choices; the True / False technique is useful here. The four true answers are labeled with a T and the one false answer is labeled with an F.

(A) CORRECT. False. This choice contradicts information given in the first paragraph: the center of percussion is only one of two sweet spots which minimize vibration. The vibration node is the other sweet spot.

(B) True. The third sentence of the first paragraph introduces the concept that the impact can "strain" the player's arm.

(C) True. The second paragraph describes at least two different forces that act upon a tennis racket striking the ball: translational as described in the second and third sentences and rotational as described in the fourth and fifth sentences.

(D) True. The fourth sentence of the second paragraph states that "unless the ball happened to hit the racket precisely at the racket's center of mass, the racket would additionally experience a rotational motion." The fifth sentence then reads, "The effect of this rotational motion would be to jerk the end of the handle forward, towards the ball."

(E) True. The second sentence of the second paragraph states that a racket will "bounce backward" after striking the ball; these words are synonyms for "rebound."

3. **What is the primary function served by paragraph two in the context of the entire passage?**

(A) to establish the main idea of the passage
(B) to provide an explanation of the mechanics of the phenomenon discussed in the passage
(C) to introduce a counterargument that elucidates the main idea of the passage

*Manhattan*GMAT®Prep

(D) to provide an example of the primary subject described in the passage

(E) to explain why the main idea of the passage would be useful for tennis players

Paragraph two introduces and explains, in great detail, the forces that act on a racket when
striking a ball. It specifically explains the means by which the "lesser-known" sweet spot, the
center of percussion, functions.

(A) The main idea is established in the first paragraph: there is a second sweet spot that results
in minimal vibration when a tennis racket strikes a ball. The second paragraph explains the
forces that affect how this second sweet spot functions; it does not itself establish the main
idea of the passage.

(B) CORRECT. This matches the description of the second paragraph above: it explains the
mechanics of the second sweet spot in great detail.

(C) The second paragraph introduces the forces that act on a racket when striking a ball, and the
concept of a center of percussion is explained. The first paragraph indicates the existence
of the center of percussion; therefore, it would be incorrect to refer to the second paragraph
as a counterargument.

(D) While the second paragraph does provide an example, this is not an example of the center
of percussion, which is the primary subject described in the passage. The example helps to
explain the forces behind the center of percussion, but is not itself an example of a center of
percussion.

(E) The first and third paragraphs, not the second paragraph, make reference to why tennis
players would want to know about the sweet spot: to minimize strain on the arm.

4. The author mentions "a penny that has been struck near its edge" in
order to

(A) show how the center of mass causes the racket to spin

(B) argue that a penny spins in the exact way that a tennis racket spins

(C) explain how translational motion works

(D) provide an illustration of a concept

(E) demonstrate that pennies and tennis rackets do not spin in the same way

The full sentence expressed in the passage is "the racket would additionally experience a rotational motion around its center of mass - much as a penny that has been struck near its edge
will start to spin." In other words, the motion of the penny is an example that closely mimics
the situation with the tennis racket. The correct answer should match this characterization.

(A) The center of mass does not cause the racket to spin; rather, a ball striking the racket causes
it to spin.

(B) The author does not present the information about the penny as an argument; rather, it is an example. In addition, the author implies, via the words "much as" that the penny and the racket spin in similar ways; this is not the same as saying that they spin in the "exact" same way.

(C) This sentence is about rotational motion, not translational motion.

(D) CORRECT. The example of the penny is a metaphor for the rotational motion experienced by the tennis racket.

(E) The example is intended to demonstrate a situation in which tennis rackets and pennies do spin in the same way.

5. Which of the following can be inferred from the passage?

> (A) If a player holds the tennis racket anywhere other than the end of the handle, the player will experience a jolting sensation.
> (B) The primary sweet spot is more effective at damping vibration than the secondary sweet spot.
> (C) Striking a tennis ball at a spot other than the center of percussion can result in a jarring feeling.
> (D) Striking a tennis ball repeatedly at spots other than a sweet spot leads to "tennis elbow."
> (E) If a player lets go of the racket at the moment of impact, the simultaneous forward and backward impetus causes the racket to drop straight to the ground.

Because the question applies to the whole passage, we must examine the answer choices first. It is useful to remember that when the GMAT asks us to "infer," we need to base our inference only on information presented in the passage.

(A) The passage does explain that holding the racket at the end of the handle and hitting the ball at a particular spot results in a comfortable stroke that reduces the strain on a player's arm. It does not address, however, what would happen if the player grasped the racket at a different point. It is possible that grasping the racket at another point would simply result in a different center of percussion.

(B) The passage states that there is one commonly known sweet spot and a second, lesser-known sweet spot. However, the passage says nothing about the relative efficacies of these two sweet spots.

(C) CORRECT. We're told that playing tennis can result in strain on a player's arm. We're also told that striking the ball at the center of percussion leads to a "smooth, comfortable stroke" or one which does not cause the same kind of damage as a "regular" stroke. Striking the ball at a spot other than the center of percussion then, could lead to a jarring stroke, or one that could cause damage to a player's arm.

(D) The passage mentions nothing about "tennis elbow" or what behavior can result in this injury; it merely talks about "strain." Be careful not to add additional information beyond what is presented in the passage.

(E) The second paragraph obliquely addresses a situation where a tennis player lets go of the racket at the moment of impact. However, this question does not specify the point at which the tennis ball struck the racket; if the ball did not strike a sweet spot, the racket may have some translational or rotational force transferred from the ball.

Answers to Passage G: Chaos Theory

Around 1960, mathematician Edward Lorenz found unexpected behavior in apparently simple equations representing atmospheric air flows. Whenever he reran his model with the same inputs, different outputs resulted – although the model lacked any random elements. Lorenz realized that tiny rounding errors in his analog computer mushroomed over time, leading to erratic results. His findings marked a seminal moment in the development of chaos theory, which, despite its name, has little to do with randomness.

To understand how unpredictability can arise from deterministic equations, which do not involve chance outcomes, consider the non-chaotic system of two poppy seeds placed in a round bowl. As the seeds roll to the bowl's center, a position known as a point attractor, the distance between the seeds shrinks. If, instead, the bowl is flipped over, two seeds placed on top will roll away from each other. Such a system, while still not technically chaotic, enlarges initial differences in position.

Chaotic systems, such as a machine mixing bread dough, are characterized by both attraction and repulsion. As the dough is stretched, folded and pressed back together, any poppy seeds sprinkled in are intermixed seemingly at random. But this randomness is illusory. In fact, the poppy seeds are captured by "strange attractors," staggeringly complex pathways whose tangles appear accidental but are in fact determined by the system's fundamental equations.

During the dough-kneading process, two poppy seeds positioned next to each other eventually go their separate ways. Any early divergence or measurement error is repeatedly amplified by the mixing until the position of any seed becomes effectively unpredictable. It is this "sensitive dependence on initial conditions" and not true randomness that generates unpredictability in chaotic systems, of which one example may be the Earth's weather. According to the popular interpretation of the "Butterfly Effect," a butterfly flapping its wings causes hurricanes. A better understanding is that the butterfly causes uncertainty about the precise state of the air. This microscopic uncertainty grows until it encompasses even hurricanes. Few meteorologists believe that we will ever be able to predict rain or shine for a particular day years in the future.

This is a LONG passage (more than 35 lines on page). Here is a model Skeletal Sketch:

> 1960, L found unexpected behavior in equations for air flows
> Reran model with same inputs, but different results
> L realized that tiny rounding errors grew over time → erratic results
> <u>Findings were imp to development of CT, little to do with chaos</u>
>
> Though non-chaotic, 2 poppy seed in round bowl enlarge initial difference of position
>
> In mixing of dough, movement of seeds seems random but is not
>
> Sensitive dependence on initial conditions, not true randomness, generates unpredictability in chaotic systems

1. The main purpose of this passage is to

    (A) explain complicated aspects of certain physical systems
    (B) trace the historical development of a scientific theory
    (C) distinguish a mathematical pattern from its opposite
    (D) describe the spread of a technical model from one field of study to others
    (E) contrast possible causes of weather phenomena

The passage's main purpose can be determined by examining the role of each paragraph. The first paragraph introduces chaos theory by describing a historical moment in its development. The next three paragraphs focus on explaining a mysterious aspect of chaotic systems: namely, the way in which "unpredictability can arise from deterministic equations, which do not involve chance outcomes," as the first sentence of the second paragraph states. These paragraphs use analogies involving poppy seeds and bread dough to illustrate the explanations. Finally, as a minor addendum, the last paragraph mentions how this understanding of chaos theory might be applied to the weather, as a possible specific case of a chaotic system.

Taking all of these roles together, we see that the main purpose of the passage is to introduce chaos theory and explain how chaotic systems seem to be random but actually are governed by very complex equations.

(A) CORRECT. The "complicated aspects" are the characteristic features of chaotic systems, such as "sensitive dependence on initial conditions." The point of the passage is to explain such features.

(B) The first paragraph, as an introduction, describes a particular milestone in the historical development of chaos theory. However, the passage does not go on to describe other developments of this theory over time.

(C) Perhaps the behavior of chaotic systems could arguably be described as a "mathematical

pattern." However, the passage does not discuss any category of systems that are categorized as the opposite of chaotic systems.

(D) If chaos theory is the "technical model" mentioned in the answer choice, the passage never describes how that model spreads from one field of study to any other.

(E) Late in the fourth paragraph, the "Butterfly Effect" is mentioned as a popular explanation for at least some hurricanes. However, no other causes of weather phenomena are ever discussed.

2. In the example discussed in the passage, what is true about poppy seeds in bread dough, once the dough has been thoroughly mixed?

(A) They have been individually stretched and folded over, like miniature versions of the entire dough.
(B) They are scattered in random clumps throughout the dough.
(C) They are accidentally caught in tangled objects called strange attractors.
(D) They are bound to regularly dispersed patterns of point attractors.
(E) They are in positions dictated by the underlying equations that govern the mixing process.

The question asks about the poppy seeds in mixed bread dough. The third paragraph describes what happens to these poppy seeds: they "are intermixed seemingly at random." But the positions of the seeds are not random, as the next sentences emphasize. Rather, the seeds "are captured by 'strange attractors,' staggeringly complex pathways whose tangles... are in fact determined by the system's fundamental equations." Thus, the positions of the seeds are themselves "determined by the system's fundamental equations."

(A) The passage mentions nothing about any stretching or folding of the poppy seeds themselves.

(B) The poppy seeds are scattered throughout the dough, but not in random clumps.

(C) The poppy seeds are caught in strange attractors, but there is nothing "accidental" about their capture. Moreover, the strange attractors described in the passage are not physical objects but rather mathematical pathways.

(D) Point attractors are not mentioned in relation to the dough-mixing process. Also, the poppy seeds, which have been "intermixed seemingly at random," are not placed at regular intervals.

(E) CORRECT. The poppy seeds may seem to be scattered at random, but they follow the pathways of the strange attractors. These pathways, and thus the seeds' positions, have been "determined by the system's fundamental equations."

3. According to the passage, the rounding errors in Lorenz's model

(A) indicated that the model was programmed in a fundamentally faulty way
(B) were deliberately included to represent tiny fluctuations in atmospheric air currents
(C) were imperceptibly small at first, but tended to grow
(D) were at least partially expected, given the complexity of the actual atmosphere
(E) shrank to insignificant levels during each trial of the model

The question asks for specific details with the keywords "rounding errors" and "Lorenz's model." The reference to Lorenz leads to the first paragraph, which contains the following sentence: "Lorenz realized that tiny rounding errors in his analog computer mushroomed over time, leading to erratic results." In other words, the rounding errors started out small but became larger.

Because the question uses the words "according to the passage," we should not try to draw any kind of inference. Rather, we should look for an answer that matches as closely as possible to the statements in the passage.

(A) Although these rounding errors are in fact "errors," nothing in the passage indicates or implies that the model overall was built incorrectly.

(B) The errors were not deliberately included in the model. We know this from the passage's first sentence, which states that Lorenz found "unexpected behavior" in his model. It may be argued that the role of these errors is similar to the role of "tiny fluctuations in atmospheric air currents" – that is, they both introduce uncertainty that grows over time. However, this answer choice claims incorrectly that the errors were inserted on purpose.

(C) CORRECT. This answer choice corresponds very closely to the statement in the passage. Some synonyms have been used, but the meaning is the same: "were imperceptibly small at first" substitutes for "tiny," and "tended to grow" substitutes for "mushroomed over time."

(D) The passage indicates that the behavior of the model was unexpected. Nothing in the passage indicates that Lorenz expected the errors at all.

(E) The errors did not shrink but rather "mushroomed over time."

4. The passage mentions each of the following as an example or potential example of a chaotic or non-chaotic system EXCEPT

(A) a dough-mixing machine
(B) atmospheric weather patterns
(C) poppy seeds placed on top of an upside-down bowl
(D) poppy seeds placed in a right-side-up bowl
(E) fluctuating butterfly flight patterns

The passage mentions several examples of systems, both chaotic and non-chaotic, to illustrate the special characteristics of chaos. This question is an exercise in finding the references to the four wrong answers quickly.

(A) A dough-mixing machine is first mentioned at the beginning of the third paragraph as an example of chaos in action: "Chaotic systems, such as a machine mixing bread dough..."

(B) Atmospheric weather patterns as a system to be studied are mentioned in both the first and the last paragraphs. In the last paragraph, the passage states that the Earth's weather may be an example of a chaotic system.

(C) Poppy seeds placed on an upside-down bowl are described in the second paragraph as an example of a non-chaotic system that creates divergence.

(D) Poppy seeds placed in a bowl that is right-side-up are described in the second paragraph as an example of a non-chaotic system that creates convergence.

(E) CORRECT. Butterfly flight patterns are nowhere mentioned as a system. According to the last paragraph, the "Butterfly Effect" is caused by the flapping of a single butterfly's wings to potentially affect atmospheric systems.

> **5. It can be inferred from the passage that which of the following pairs of items would most likely follow typical pathways within a chaotic system?**
>
> (A) two particles ejected in random directions from the same decaying atomic nucleus
> (B) two stickers affixed to a balloon that expands and contracts over and over again
> (C) two avalanches sliding down opposite sides of the same mountain
> (D) two baseballs placed into an active tumble dryer
> (E) two coins flipped into a large bowl

Stripped down to its essence, the question asks you to infer which of the five choices describes a system that is the most "chaotic," according to the characteristics of chaos outlined in the passage. The most important proof sentence is at the beginning of the third paragraph: "Chaotic systems, such as a machine mixing bread dough, are characterized by both attraction and repulsion." Thus, you should look for the system that is the most analogous to the dough-mixing machine. Moreover, the system should contain both attractive and repulsive elements: in other words, the two items embedded within the system should sometimes come near each other and then separate again.

At the beginning of the fourth paragraph, there is a "red herring" proof sentence: "During the dough-kneading process, two poppy seeds positioned next to each other eventually go their separate ways." This sentence could lead you to think that the defining characteristic of chaotic systems is simply that two embedded items move away from each other. The question is asked in such a way as to focus your attention on the two items, so that you might then use this proof sentence alone and choose an incorrect answer.

(A) The two particles ejected from a nucleus do diverge, but they do not approach each other again. Moreover, there is no implication of any activity analogous to mixing bread dough.

(B) The stickers on the balloon separate and come together repeatedly. This behavior meets the criterion of "both attraction and repulsion." However, there is no mixing, and as a result, the system cannot be said to be analogous to a machine mixing dough.

(C) As in answer choice (A), the two items in question (avalanches) separate but never draw near each other again. Likewise, there is no mixing in the system.

(D) CORRECT. Two baseballs placed into an active tumble dryer are analogous to two poppy seeds placed in bread dough being mixed by a machine: parts of the system are separated, intermingled and brought back together again in perfectly regular, though complex, ways. The pathways of the two baseballs will diverge and converge repeatedly, as in any other chaotic system.

(E) The two coins flipped into a bowl is closely analogous to the example in the second paragraph of the passage of two poppy seeds placed in a bowl and allowed to fall; this system is presented as non-chaotic.

REAL GMAT PASSAGES & QUESTIONS

Now that you have completed your study of READING COMPREHENSION, it is time to test your skills on passages that have actually appeared on real GMAT exams over the past several years. These passages can be found in two books published by GMAC (Graduate Management Admission Council):

The Official Guide for GMAT Review, 11th Edition (pages 26-31 & 346-393) and
The Official Guide for GMAT Verbal Review (pages 22-56)

Read each passage in the Reading Comprehension section of the two books above and answer all the questions associated with each passage using the following guidelines:

1) Before you read each passage, identify whether it is LONG or SHORT. (LONG passages are those with more than 35 lines on the page. SHORT passages are those with 35 lines or fewer.)

2) Preview the first question before reading, but do not look at any of the subsequent questions prior to reading the passage, since you will not be able to do this on the GMAT.

3) As you read the passage, create a Headline List (for SHORT passages) or a Skeletal Sketch (for LONG passages). Then, use your Headline List or Skeletal Sketch to assist you in answering all the questions that accompany the passage.

4) Before answering each question, identify it as either a General question or a Specific question. Use the 7 strategies for Reading Comprehension to assist you in answering the questions.

5) On the GMAT, you will typically see 3 questions on SHORT passages and 4 questions on LONG passages. However, in *The Official Guides*, the number of questions that you will see for each particular passage will vary significantly. As such, use the following MODIFIED timing guidelines during your practice:

For Short Passages: Spend approximately 2 to 3 minutes reading and creating your Headline List. Spend approximately 60 seconds answering General questions and between 60 to 90 seconds answering Specific questions.

For Long Passages: Spend approximately 3 minutes reading and creating your Skeletal Sketch. Spend approximately 60 seconds answering General questions and between 60 to 90 seconds answering Specific questions.

In general, simply use the following timing formula for each passage:

(# of Questions) x 2 = Total # of Minutes You Should Spend

This total number of minutes includes time for reading the passage, creating a Headline List or Skeletal Sketch, and answering all the questions.

To waive "Finance I" at Harvard Business School you must:
    (A) Be a CFA
    (B) Have prior coursework in finance
    (C) Have two years of relevant work experience in the financial sector
    (D) Pass a waiver exam
    (E) None of the above; one cannot waive core courses at HBS

What are the requirements of an Entrepreneurial Management major at the Wharton School?
    (1) Completion of 5 credit units (cu) that qualify for the major
    (2) Participation in the Wharton Business Plan Competition during the 2nd year of the MBA program
(A) Statement (1) ALONE is sufficient, but statement (2) alone is not sufficient.
(B) Statement (2) ALONE is sufficient, but statement (1) alone is not sufficient.
(C) BOTH statements TOGETHER are sufficient, but NEITHER statement ALONE is sufficient.
(D) EACH statement ALONE is sufficient.
(E) Statements (1) and (2) TOGETHER are NOT sufficient.

Once You Ace the GMAT, Get Ready to Ace Your Applications!

To make an informed decision in applying to a school—and to craft an effective application that demonstrates an appreciation of a program's unique merits—**it's crucial that you do your homework**. Clear Admit School Guides cut through the gloss of marketing materials to give you the hard facts about a program, and then put these school-specific details in context so you can see how programs compare. In the guides, you'll find detailed, comparative information on vital topics such as:

- The core curriculum and first-year experience
- Leading professors in key fields
- Student clubs and conferences
- Full-time job placement by industry and location
- Student demographics
- International and experiential learning programs
- Tuition, financial aid and scholarships
- Admissions deadlines and procedures

Now available for top schools including:
Chicago, Columbia, Harvard, Kellogg, MIT, Stanford, Tuck and Wharton

A time-saving source of comprehensive information, Clear Admit School Guides have been featured in *The Economist* and lauded by applicants, business school students and MBA graduates:

"**Purchasing the Clear Admit HBS School Guide was one of best decisions I made.** I visited HBS three times and have every book and pamphlet that covers the top business schools, but nothing can compare to the Clear Admit guides in offering up-to-date information on every aspect of the school's academic and social life that is not readily available on the school's website and brochures. Reading a Clear Admit School Guide gives an applicant the necessary, detailed school information to be competitive in the application process."
—An applicant to Harvard

CLEAR ADMIT
School Guides

"I want to tip my hat to the team at Clear Admit that put these guides together. I'm a recent graduate of Wharton's MBA program and remain active in the admissions process (serving as an alumni interviewer to evaluate applicants). I can't tell you how important it is for applicants to show genuine enthusiasm for Wharton and I think the Clear Admit School Guide for Wharton captures many of the important details, as well as the spirit of the school. **This sort of information is a must for the serious MBA applicant.**"
—A Wharton MBA graduate

Question #1: (e) and Question #2 (a)

www.clearadmit.com/schoolguides

contact us at mbaguides@clearadmit.com

Finally, a GMAT* prep guide series that goes beyond the basics.

Reading Comprehension, 2007 Edition
ISBN: 978-0-9790175-6-8
Retail: $26

Critical Reasoning, 2007 Edition
ISBN: 978-0-9790175-5-1
Retail: $26

Word Translations, 2007 Edition
ISBN: 978-0-9790175-3-7
Retail: $26

Number Properties, 2007 Edition
ISBN: 978-0-9790175-0-6
Retail: $26

Geometry, 2007 Edition
ISBN: 978-0-9790175-4-4
Retail: $26

Equations, Inequalities, & VIC's, 2007 Edition
ISBN: 978-0-9790175-2-0
Retail: $26

Sentence Correction, 2007 Edition
ISBN: 978-0-9790175-7-5
Retail: $26

Fractions, Decimals, & Percents, 2007 Edition
ISBN: 978-0-9790175-1-3
Retail: $26

Published by

Manhattan **GMAT***Prep

✔ You get many more pages per topic than found in all-in-one tomes.

✔ Only buy those guides that address the specific skills you need to develop.

✔ Gain access to Online Practice GMAT* Exams & bonus question banks.

COMMENTS FROM GMAT TEST TAKERS:

Now Available at your local bookstore!

"Bravo, Manhattan GMAT! Bravo! The guides truly did not disappoint. All the guides are clear, concise, and well organized and explained things in a manner that made it possible to understand things the first time through without missing any of the important details."

"I've thumbed through a lot of books that don't even touch these. The fact that they're split up into components is immeasurably helpful. The set-up of each guide and the lists of past GMAT problems make for an incredibly thorough and easy to follow study path."

*GMAT and GMAC are registered trademarks of the Graduate Management Admission Council which neither sponsors nor endorses this product.